A 365-DAY JOU|

Gratitude, Positivity & Self-Love

TO TRANSFORM YOUR MINDSET AND TRANSFORM YOUR LIFE

This journal belongs to

_____

Start Date

_____

Start your Day with Gratitude

*"Gratitude is
the
Great Magnifier."*

RHONDA BYRNE

Every morning, set the energy for your day by listing ten things that you are grateful for and really *feel the feeling* of gratitude! You will carry this positive energy with you throughout the day, and day-by-day, you will feel happier, more positive and more receptive to the good that you desire.

Noticing the Good is a powerful practice that brings more joy to your life and to the lives of those around you. By transforming yourself into a person of gratitude, you will start noticing more things to be grateful for. As you notice the good things that already exist in yourself and all around you, you will start to expect to see more things to be grateful for. This positive expectancy opens the door for more good to flow to you and through you.

Every morning, putting pen to paper and writing down ten things you are grateful for, sends a strong signal to your subconscious mind that aids in the repatterning of thoughts and beliefs. Moment by moment, day by day, build your life into a life of gratitude and enjoy the benefits of this powerful practice.

Daily Self-Image

"You can never out-perform your own self-image, but you can change it."

MAXWELL MALTZ

Your self-image is up to you. You are the one who has the power to be the person you want to be. As you begin each day, decide who you are going to be, and be that person throughout the day.

Here are some useful questions to ask yourself:

- Who do I want to be today?
- What energy do I want to radiate today?
- What story am I practicing today?
- What mindset do I want to adopt today?
- What attitude do I want to take on today?
- What qualities do I want to step into today?

By making this a daily morning practice, you are taking the important steps to intentionally create, design and be the person you want to become.

Inspired Action

"Inspiration without action is merely entertainment. Act on your inspiration today."

MARY MORRISSEY

Wake up each morning with enthusiasm about the day you are about to create! You are the creator of each moment, each day, and ultimately of your entire life.

A very powerful practice is to think of six goal-orientated actions you would love to take... and write these down the night before. This way, you've already set your intention the night before to take the inspired actions you'd love to take the following day.

Here are some powerful questions to ask yourself:
- What would I love to do?
- What would I love to have?
- What would I love to give?
- What would I love to create?

When you awake in the morning, your mind will be set and inspired to take action on the energizing goals you have laid out in front of you. Your life is up to you! Go ahead, and be the intentional creator of your life!

Sending Love

"There is no love without forgiveness, and there is no forgiveness without love."

BRYANT H. McGILL

Each morning, think about three people you would love to forgive or people that you want to send loving vibrations to. Write their names down, and send them love by thinking this:

- May you be truly happy.
- May you live in peace.
- May you live in love.
- May you know the power of forgiveness.
- May you live in recognition that your life has deep meaning, and good purpose.

Forgiveness and sending love to others is a powerful practice of Self-Love. The more you get onto this frequency of love, the more love you attract into your own life.

Positive Affirmations

"Whatever we plant in our subconscious mind and nourish with repetition and emotion will become a reality."

EARL NIGHTINGALE

Thoughts become things. It is powerful to get connected to this truth so that we can begin to think intentionally about what we want to consciously create.

There is a saying that *everything is created twice*. This means that before something takes form in the 3D world, it is first created as a thought-form in the mind.

This fundamental principle is true for all thoughts. Positive thoughts become things, and the same is true for negative thoughts. This is where the power of positive affirmations comes in. Our subconscious mind is fertile soil for any type of thought we want to plant in it. So, we can plant thought seeds that we want to flourish in our minds, knowing that they will become things. When we do this repeatedly over time and get emotionally involved with the thought, we are able to transform ourselves in a way that is in alignment with the good that we desire.

Discover the power of the positive affirmations in this journal, and enjoy your 365-day journey of gratitude, positivity and self-love!

Gratitude

Today, I am so happy and grateful for...

1 _____ 6 _____
2 _____ 7 _____
3 _____ 8 _____
4 _____ 9 _____
5 _____ 10 _____

Self-Image

Today, I am...

_____
_____
_____

Inspired Action

Today, I take these actions towards my goals...

1 _____ 4 _____
2 _____ 5 _____
3 _____ 6 _____

Sending Love

Today, I send love to these people in my life...

1 _____
2 _____
3 _____

Powerful Positive Affirmation

I AM WHOLE, STRONG, POWERFUL, LOVING, HARMONIOUS AND HAPPY.

Gratitude

Today, I am so happy and grateful for...

1 _____   6 _____

2 _____   7 _____

3 _____   8 _____

4 _____   9 _____

5 _____   10 _____

Self-Image

Today, I am...

_____

_____

_____

Inspired Action

Today, I take these actions towards my goals...

1 _____   4 _____

2 _____   5 _____

3 _____   6 _____

Sending Love

Today, I send love to these people in my life...

1 _____

2 _____

3 _____

Powerful Positive Affirmation

I AM A MAGNET FOR THE HEALTH, WEALTH AND HAPPINESS I DESIRE.

Gratitude

Today, I am so happy and grateful for...

1 _____   6 _____

2 _____   7 _____

3 _____   8 _____

4 _____   9 _____

5 _____   10 _____

Self-Image

Today, I am...

_____

_____

_____

Inspired Action

Today, I take these actions towards my goals...

1 _____   4 _____

2 _____   5 _____

3 _____   6 _____

Sending Love

Today, I send love to these people in my life...

1 _____

2 _____

3 _____

Powerful Positive Affirmation

I AM A POWERFUL MANIFESTOR.

Gratitude
Today, I am so happy and grateful for...

1 _____
2 _____
3 _____
4 _____
5 _____

6 _____
7 _____
8 _____
9 _____
10 _____

Self-Image
Today, I am...

_____
_____
_____

Inspired Action
Today, I take these actions towards my goals...

1 _____
2 _____
3 _____

4 _____
5 _____
6 _____

Sending Love
Today, I send love to these people in my life...

1 _____
2 _____
3 _____

Powerful Positive Affirmation

I AM IN CHARGE OF MY OWN HAPPINESS.

Gratitude
Today, I am so happy and grateful for...

1 _____
2 _____
3 _____
4 _____
5 _____

6 _____
7 _____
8 _____
9 _____
10 _____

Self-Image
Today, I am...

_____

_____

_____

Inspired Action
Today, I take these actions towards my goals...

1 _____
2 _____
3 _____

4 _____
5 _____
6 _____

Sending Love
Today, I send love to these people in my life...

1 _____
2 _____
3 _____

Powerful Positive Affirmation

I ACCEPT 100% RESPONSIBILITY FOR MY OWN LIFE.

Gratitude

Today, I am so happy and grateful for...

1 _____   6 _____

2 _____   7 _____

3 _____   8 _____

4 _____   9 _____

5 _____   10 _____

Self-Image

Today, I am...

_____

_____

_____

Inspired Action

Today, I take these actions towards my goals...

1 _____   4 _____

2 _____   5 _____

3 _____   6 _____

Sending Love

Today, I send love to these people in my life...

1 _____

2 _____

3 _____

Powerful Positive Affirmation

I SEE MY FUTURE SELF JUMPING FOR JOY SAYING, "THANK YOU! THANK YOU! THANK YOU!"

Gratitude

Today, I am so happy and grateful for...

1 _____ 6 _____

2 _____ 7 _____

3 _____ 8 _____

4 _____ 9 _____

5 _____ 10 _____

Self-Image

Today, I am...

_____

_____

_____

Inspired Action

Today, I take these actions towards my goals...

1 _____ 4 _____

2 _____ 5 _____

3 _____ 6 _____

Sending Love

Today, I send love to these people in my life...

1 _____

2 _____

3 _____

Powerful Positive Affirmation

I ONLY FOCUS ON WHAT I WANT.

Gratitude
Today, I am so happy and grateful for...

1 _____   6 _____

2 _____   7 _____

3 _____   8 _____

4 _____   9 _____

5 _____   10 _____

Self-Image
Today, I am...

_____

_____

_____

Inspired Action
Today, I take these actions towards my goals...

1 _____   4 _____

2 _____   5 _____

3 _____   6 _____

Sending Love
Today, I send love to these people in my life...

1 _____

2 _____

3 _____

Powerful Positive Affirmation

MY TRUE, AUTHENTIC, INNER SELF
KNOWS WHAT I WANT.

Gratitude
Today, I am so happy and grateful for...

1 _____   6 _____
2 _____   7 _____
3 _____   8 _____
4 _____   9 _____
5 _____   10 _____

Self-Image
Today, I am...

_____
_____
_____

Inspired Action
Today, I take these actions towards my goals...

1 _____   4 _____
2 _____   5 _____
3 _____   6 _____

Sending Love
Today, I send love to these people in my life...

1 _____
2 _____
3 _____

Powerful Positive Affirmation

I AM IN TOUCH WITH MY INTUITION.

Gratitude
Today, I am so happy and grateful for...

1 _____   6 _____
2 _____   7 _____
3 _____   8 _____
4 _____   9 _____
5 _____   10 _____

Self-Image
Today, I am...

_____

_____

_____

Inspired Action
Today, I take these actions towards my goals...

1 _____   4 _____
2 _____   5 _____
3 _____   6 _____

Sending Love
Today, I send love to these people in my life...

1 _____
2 _____
3 _____

Powerful Positive Affirmation

EVERYTHING IN MY LIFE HAPPENS FOR ME.

Gratitude

Today, I am so happy and grateful for...

1 _____   6 _____
2 _____   7 _____
3 _____   8 _____
4 _____   9 _____
5 _____   10 _____

Self-Image

Today, I am...

_____

_____

_____

Inspired Action

Today, I take these actions towards my goals...

1 _____   4 _____
2 _____   5 _____
3 _____   6 _____

Sending Love

Today, I send love to these people in my life...

1 _____
2 _____
3 _____

Powerful Positive Affirmation

THE CONTENT OF MY LIFE IS
THE CURRICULUM OF MY EVOLUTION.

Gratitude

Today, I am so happy and grateful for...

1 _____   6 _____

2 _____   7 _____

3 _____   8 _____

4 _____   9 _____

5 _____   10 _____

Self-Image
Today, I am...

_____

_____

_____

Inspired Action
Today, I take these actions towards my goals...

1 _____   4 _____

2 _____   5 _____

3 _____   6 _____

Sending Love
Today, I send love to these people in my life...

1 _____

2 _____

3 _____

Powerful Positive Affirmation

I AM WORTHY OF WHAT I DESIRE.

Gratitude
Today, I am so happy and grateful for...

1 _____
2 _____
3 _____
4 _____
5 _____

6 _____
7 _____
8 _____
9 _____
10 _____

Self-Image
Today, I am...

_____

_____

_____

Inspired Action
Today, I take these actions towards my goals...

1 _____
2 _____
3 _____

4 _____
5 _____
6 _____

Sending Love
Today, I send love to these people in my life...

1 _____
2 _____
3 _____

Powerful Positive Affirmation

I AM THE HERO OF MY OWN LIFE.

Gratitude

Today, I am so happy and grateful for...

1 _____   6 _____
2 _____   7 _____
3 _____   8 _____
4 _____   9 _____
5 _____   10 _____

Self-Image
Today, I am...

_____

_____

_____

Inspired Action
Today, I take these actions towards my goals...

1 _____   4 _____
2 _____   5 _____
3 _____   6 _____

Sending Love
Today, I send love to these people in my life...

1 _____
2 _____
3 _____

Powerful Positive Affirmation

THINGS ARE FALLING PERFECTLY INTO PLACE WITH MORE OPPORTUNITY, SUCCESS AND JOY THAN EVER BEFORE.

Gratitude
Today, I am so happy and grateful for...

1 _____   6 _____

2 _____   7 _____

3 _____   8 _____

4 _____   9 _____

5 _____   10 _____

Self-Image
Today, I am...

_____

_____

_____

Inspired Action
Today, I take these actions towards my goals...

1 _____   4 _____

2 _____   5 _____

3 _____   6 _____

Sending Love
Today, I send love to these people in my life...

1 _____

2 _____

3 _____

Powerful Positive Affirmation

GREAT OPPORTUNITIES ARE HAPPENING IN MY LIFE.

Gratitude

Today, I am so happy and grateful for...

1 _____   6 _____

2 _____   7 _____

3 _____   8 _____

4 _____   9 _____

5 _____   10 _____

Self-Image

Today, I am...

_____

_____

_____

Inspired Action

Today, I take these actions towards my goals...

1 _____   4 _____

2 _____   5 _____

3 _____   6 _____

Sending Love

Today, I send love to these people in my life...

1 _____

2 _____

3 _____

Powerful Positive Affirmation

MONEY IS COMING TO ME IN INCREASING AMOUNTS THROUGH MULTIPLE SOURCES ON A CONTINUOUS BASIS.

Gratitude
Today, I am so happy and grateful for...

1 _____   6 _____

2 _____   7 _____

3 _____   8 _____

4 _____   9 _____

5 _____   10 _____

Self-Image
Today, I am...

_____

_____

_____

Inspired Action
Today, I take these actions towards my goals...

1 _____   4 _____

2 _____   5 _____

3 _____   6 _____

Sending Love
Today, I send love to these people in my life...

1 _____

2 _____

3 _____

Powerful Positive Affirmation

MY LIFE IS FULL OF LOVE.
I LOVE WHO I AM,
I LOVE WHAT I AM DOING,
AND I LOVE WHAT I AM BECOMING.

Gratitude

Today, I am so happy and grateful for...

1 _____   6 _____

2 _____   7 _____

3 _____   8 _____

4 _____   9 _____

5 _____   10 _____

Self-Image

Today, I am...

_____

_____

_____

Inspired Action

Today, I take these actions towards my goals...

1 _____   4 _____

2 _____   5 _____

3 _____   6 _____

Sending Love

Today, I send love to these people in my life...

1 _____

2 _____

3 _____

Powerful Positive Affirmation

ABUNDANCE FLOWS TO ME
MORE AND MORE EVERYDAY.

Gratitude

Day   Month   Year

Today, I am so happy and grateful for...

1 _____   6 _____

2 _____   7 _____

3 _____   8 _____

4 _____   9 _____

5 _____   10 _____

Self-Image

Today, I am...

_____

_____

_____

Inspired Action

Today, I take these actions towards my goals...

1 _____   4 _____

2 _____   5 _____

3 _____   6 _____

Sending Love

Today, I send love to these people in my life...

1 _____

2 _____

3 _____

Powerful Positive Affirmation

EVERY DAY, IN EVERY WAY,
I AM GROWING MORE AND MORE CONFIDENT.

Gratitude

Today, I am so happy and grateful for...

1 _____   6 _____
2 _____   7 _____
3 _____   8 _____
4 _____   9 _____
5 _____   10 _____

Self-Image

Today, I am...

_____

_____

_____

Inspired Action

Today, I take these actions towards my goals...

1 _____   4 _____
2 _____   5 _____
3 _____   6 _____

Sending Love

Today, I send love to these people in my life...

1 _____
2 _____
3 _____

Powerful Positive Affirmation

EVERY DAY, IN EVERY WAY,
I AM APPROACHING MY IDEAL WEIGHT.

Gratitude
Today, I am so happy and grateful for...

1 _____   6 _____
2 _____   7 _____
3 _____   8 _____
4 _____   9 _____
5 _____   10 _____

Self-Image
Today, I am...

_____

_____

_____

Inspired Action
Today, I take these actions towards my goals...

1 _____   4 _____
2 _____   5 _____
3 _____   6 _____

Sending Love
Today, I send love to these people in my life...

1 _____
2 _____
3 _____

Powerful Positive Affirmation

EVERY DAY, I AM MORE AND MORE YOUTHFUL, VIBRANT AND RADIATING.

Gratitude
Today, I am so happy and grateful for...

1 _____   6 _____

2 _____   7 _____

3 _____   8 _____

4 _____   9 _____

5 _____   10 _____

Self-Image
Today, I am...

_____

_____

_____

Inspired Action
Today, I take these actions towards my goals...

1 _____   4 _____

2 _____   5 _____

3 _____   6 _____

Sending Love
Today, I send love to these people in my life...

1 _____

2 _____

3 _____

Powerful Positive Affirmation

I AM A MONEY MAGNET.

Gratitude
Today, I am so happy and grateful for...

1 _____
2 _____
3 _____
4 _____
5 _____

6 _____
7 _____
8 _____
9 _____
10 _____

Self-Image
Today, I am...

_____

_____

_____

Inspired Action
Today, I take these actions towards my goals...

1 _____
2 _____
3 _____

4 _____
5 _____
6 _____

Sending Love
Today, I send love to these people in my life...

1 _____
2 _____
3 _____

Powerful Positive Affirmation

I AM BRIMMING WITH ENERGY
AND OVERFLOWING WITH JOY.

Gratitude
Today, I am so happy and grateful for...

1 _____   6 _____
2 _____   7 _____
3 _____   8 _____
4 _____   9 _____
5 _____   10 _____

Self-Image
Today, I am...

_____

_____

_____

Inspired Action
Today, I take these actions towards my goals...

1 _____   4 _____
2 _____   5 _____
3 _____   6 _____

Sending Love
Today, I send love to these people in my life...

1 _____

2 _____

3 _____

Powerful Positive Affirmation

I FEEL HAPPY TO LOOK IN THE MIRROR, SAYING, "I LOVE YOU, I REALLY LOVE YOU."

Gratitude
Today, I am so happy and grateful for...

1 _____
2 _____
3 _____
4 _____
5 _____

6 _____
7 _____
8 _____
9 _____
10 _____

Self-Image
Today, I am...

_____

_____

_____

Inspired Action
Today, I take these actions towards my goals...

1 _____
2 _____
3 _____

4 _____
5 _____
6 _____

Sending Love
Today, I send love to these people in my life...

1 _____
2 _____
3 _____

Powerful Positive Affirmation

I POSSESS THE QUALITIES NEEDED TO BE EXTREMELY SUCCESSFUL.

Gratitude
Today, I am so happy and grateful for…

1 _____   6 _____

2 _____   7 _____

3 _____   8 _____

4 _____   9 _____

5 _____   10 _____

Self-Image
Today, I am…

_____

_____

_____

Inspired Action
Today, I take these actions towards my goals…

1 _____   4 _____

2 _____   5 _____

3 _____   6 _____

Sending Love
Today, I send love to these people in my life…

1 _____

2 _____

3 _____

Powerful Positive Affirmation

I CLAIM MY POWER AND MOVE BEYOND ALL LIMITATIONS.

Gratitude
Today, I am so happy and grateful for...

1 _____   6 _____

2 _____   7 _____

3 _____   8 _____

4 _____   9 _____

5 _____   10 _____

Self-Image
Today, I am...

_____

_____

_____

Inspired Action
Today, I take these actions towards my goals...

1 _____   4 _____

2 _____   5 _____

3 _____   6 _____

Sending Love
Today, I send love to these people in my life...

1 _____

2 _____

3 _____

Powerful Positive Affirmation

I AM AWARE THAT I AM LIVING IN AN OCEAN OF LOVE.

Gratitude

Today, I am so happy and grateful for...

1 _____   6 _____
2 _____   7 _____
3 _____   8 _____
4 _____   9 _____
5 _____   10 _____

Self-Image

Today, I am...

_____
_____
_____

Inspired Action

Today, I take these actions towards my goals...

1 _____   4 _____
2 _____   5 _____
3 _____   6 _____

Sending Love

Today, I send love to these people in my life...

1 _____
2 _____
3 _____

Powerful Positive Affirmation

I FEEL LOVE IN ALL THAT I DO.

Gratitude
Today, I am so happy and grateful for...

1 _____   6 _____
2 _____   7 _____
3 _____   8 _____
4 _____   9 _____
5 _____   10 _____

Self-Image
Today, I am...

_____

_____

_____

Inspired Action
Today, I take these actions towards my goals...

1 _____   4 _____
2 _____   5 _____
3 _____   6 _____

Sending Love
Today, I send love to these people in my life...

1 _____
2 _____
3 _____

Powerful Positive Affirmation

MY MIND IS A CENTRE OF DIVINE OPERATION, ALWAYS FOR EXPANSION AND FULLER EXPRESSION.

Gratitude

Today, I am so happy and grateful for...

1 _____   6 _____

2 _____   7 _____

3 _____   8 _____

4 _____   9 _____

5 _____   10 _____

Self-Image

Today, I am...

_____

_____

_____

Inspired Action

Today, I take these actions towards my goals...

1 _____   4 _____

2 _____   5 _____

3 _____   6 _____

Sending Love

Today, I send love to these people in my life...

1 _____

2 _____

3 _____

Powerful Positive Affirmation

I AM THE ARTIST OF MY REALITY. EVERY THOUGHT, FEELING AND ACTION CONTRIBUTE TO MY BEAUTIFUL LIFE.

Gratitude
Today, I am so happy and grateful for...

1 _____   6 _____

2 _____   7 _____

3 _____   8 _____

4 _____   9 _____

5 _____   10 _____

Self-Image
Today, I am...

_____

_____

_____

Inspired Action
Today, I take these actions towards my goals...

1 _____   4 _____

2 _____   5 _____

3 _____   6 _____

Sending Love
Today, I send love to these people in my life...

1 _____

2 _____

3 _____

Powerful Positive Affirmation

EVERY MOMENT IS AN OPPORTUNITY
TO START FRESH WITH A NEW PERSPECTIVE
AND POSITIVE ATTITUDE.

Gratitude
Today, I am so happy and grateful for...

1 _____   6 _____

2 _____   7 _____

3 _____   8 _____

4 _____   9 _____

5 _____   10 _____

Self-Image
Today, I am...

_____

_____

_____

Inspired Action
Today, I take these actions towards my goals...

1 _____   4 _____

2 _____   5 _____

3 _____   6 _____

Sending Love
Today, I send love to these people in my life...

1 _____

2 _____

3 _____

Powerful Positive Affirmation

ABUNDANCE, JOY AND FULFILLMENT ARE ALWAYS READILY AVAILABLE.

Gratitude

Today, I am so happy and grateful for...

1 _____   6 _____
2 _____   7 _____
3 _____   8 _____
4 _____   9 _____
5 _____   10 _____

Self-Image

Today, I am...

_____

_____

_____

Inspired Action

Today, I take these actions towards my goals...

1 _____   4 _____
2 _____   5 _____
3 _____   6 _____

Sending Love

Today, I send love to these people in my life...

1 _____
2 _____
3 _____

Powerful Positive Affirmation

EVERY DAY BRINGS NEW IDEAS, NEW INSPIRATION AND NEW OPPORTUNITIES TO LIVE MY BEST LIFE.

Gratitude
Today, I am so happy and grateful for...

1 _____   6 _____

2 _____   7 _____

3 _____   8 _____

4 _____   9 _____

5 _____   10 _____

Self-Image
Today, I am...

_____

_____

_____

_____

Inspired Action
Today, I take these actions towards my goals...

1 _____   4 _____

2 _____   5 _____

3 _____   6 _____

Sending Love
Today, I send love to these people in my life...

1 _____

2 _____

3 _____

Powerful Positive Affirmation

MY THOUGHTS ARE CREATING MY LIFE,
AND I AM RICH IN ALL
THE GOOD THINGS IN MY LIFE.

Gratitude
Today, I am so happy and grateful for...

1 _____   6 _____
2 _____   7 _____
3 _____   8 _____
4 _____   9 _____
5 _____   10 _____

Self-Image
Today, I am...

_____

_____

_____

Inspired Action
Today, I take these actions towards my goals...

1 _____   4 _____
2 _____   5 _____
3 _____   6 _____

Sending Love
Today, I send love to these people in my life...

1 _____
2 _____
3 _____

Powerful Positive Affirmation

EACH MOMENT, I HAVE AN OPPORTUNITY TO BE, DO AND HAVE ANYTHING I WANT.

Gratitude
Today, I am so happy and grateful for...

1 _____   6 _____

2 _____   7 _____

3 _____   8 _____

4 _____   9 _____

5 _____   10 _____

Self-Image
Today, I am...

_____

_____

_____

Inspired Action
Today, I take these actions towards my goals...

1 _____   4 _____

2 _____   5 _____

3 _____   6 _____

Sending Love
Today, I send love to these people in my life...

1 _____

2 _____

3 _____

Powerful Positive Affirmation

CREATIVE ENERGY SURGES THROUGH ME
AND LEADS ME TO NEW AND BRILLIANT IDEAS.

Gratitude

Today, I am so happy and grateful for...

1 _____   6 _____

2 _____   7 _____

3 _____   8 _____

4 _____   9 _____

5 _____   10 _____

Self-Image

Today, I am...

_____

_____

_____

Inspired Action

Today, I take these actions towards my goals...

1 _____   4 _____

2 _____   5 _____

3 _____   6 _____

Sending Love

Today, I send love to these people in my life...

1 _____

2 _____

3 _____

Powerful Positive Affirmation

DEEP AT THE CENTER OF MY BEING
IS AN INFINITE WELL OF LOVE.

Gratitude

Today, I am so happy and grateful for...

1 _____   6 _____
2 _____   7 _____
3 _____   8 _____
4 _____   9 _____
5 _____   10 _____

Self-Image

Today, I am...

_____

_____

_____

Inspired Action

Today, I take these actions towards my goals...

1 _____   4 _____
2 _____   5 _____
3 _____   6 _____

Sending Love

Today, I send love to these people in my life...

1 _____

2 _____

3 _____

Powerful Positive Affirmation

MY THOUGHTS ARE FILLED WITH POSITIVITY
AND MY LIFE IS PLENTIFUL WITH PROSPERITY.

Gratitude
Today, I am so happy and grateful for...

1 _____   6 _____
2 _____   7 _____
3 _____   8 _____
4 _____   9 _____
5 _____   10 _____

Self-Image
Today, I am...

_____

_____

_____

Inspired Action
Today, I take these actions towards my goals...

1 _____   4 _____
2 _____   5 _____
3 _____   6 _____

Sending Love
Today, I send love to these people in my life...

1 _____
2 _____
3 _____

Powerful Positive Affirmation

I AM LIVING IN AN ABUNDANCE OF GREAT HEALTH, INCREASING WEALTH AND THRIVING RELATIONSHIPS.

Gratitude
Today, I am so happy and grateful for...

1 _____   6 _____
2 _____   7 _____
3 _____   8 _____
4 _____   9 _____
5 _____   10 _____

Self-Image
Today, I am...

_____
_____
_____

Inspired Action
Today, I take these actions towards my goals...

1 _____   4 _____
2 _____   5 _____
3 _____   6 _____

Sending Love
Today, I send love to these people in my life...

1 _____
2 _____
3 _____

Powerful Positive Affirmation

I AM A FOUNTAIN OF ENERGY, IDEAS, INSPIRATION, POSITIVITY AND ABUNDANCE.

Gratitude

Today, I am so happy and grateful for...

1 _____
2 _____
3 _____
4 _____
5 _____

6 _____
7 _____
8 _____
9 _____
10 _____

Self-Image
Today, I am...

_____

_____

_____

Inspired Action
Today, I take these actions towards my goals...

1 _____
2 _____
3 _____

4 _____
5 _____
6 _____

Sending Love
Today, I send love to these people in my life...

1 _____
2 _____
3 _____

Powerful Positive Affirmation

I HAVE THE SELF-ESTEEM, POWER AND CONFIDENCE TO MOVE FORWARD IN LIFE WITH EASE.

Gratitude
Today, I am so happy and grateful for...

1 _____   6 _____
2 _____   7 _____
3 _____   8 _____
4 _____   9 _____
5 _____   10 _____

Self-Image
Today, I am...

_____

_____

_____

Inspired Action
Today, I take these actions towards my goals...

1 _____   4 _____
2 _____   5 _____
3 _____   6 _____

Sending Love
Today, I send love to these people in my life...

1 _____
2 _____
3 _____

Powerful Positive Affirmation

I ACCEPT AND USE MY OWN POWER
AS I TAKE ACTION ON MY GOALS.

Gratitude

Today, I am so happy and grateful for...

1 _____   6 _____

2 _____   7 _____

3 _____   8 _____

4 _____   9 _____

5 _____   10 _____

Self-Image

Today, I am...

_____

_____

_____

Inspired Action

Today, I take these actions towards my goals...

1 _____   4 _____

2 _____   5 _____

3 _____   6 _____

Sending Love

Today, I send love to these people in my life...

1 _____

2 _____

3 _____

Powerful Positive Affirmation

I AM THE MAIN CHARACTER IN THE MOVIE OF MY LIFE.

Gratitude

Today, I am so happy and grateful for...

1 _____   6 _____

2 _____   7 _____

3 _____   8 _____

4 _____   9 _____

5 _____   10 _____

Self-Image

Today, I am...

_____

_____

_____

Inspired Action

Today, I take these actions towards my goals...

1 _____   4 _____

2 _____   5 _____

3 _____   6 _____

Sending Love

Today, I send love to these people in my life...

1 _____

2 _____

3 _____

Powerful Positive Affirmation

I AM MY LIGHT.

Gratitude

Today, I am so happy and grateful for...

1 _____ 6 _____
2 _____ 7 _____
3 _____ 8 _____
4 _____ 9 _____
5 _____ 10 _____

Self-Image

Today, I am...

_____
_____
_____

Inspired Action

Today, I take these actions towards my goals...

1 _____ 4 _____
2 _____ 5 _____
3 _____ 6 _____

Sending Love

Today, I send love to these people in my life...

1 _____
2 _____
3 _____

Powerful Positive Affirmation

I AM THE ARCHITECT OF MY LIFE; I BUILD ITS FOUNDATION AND CHOOSE ITS CONTENTS.

Gratitude

Today, I am so happy and grateful for...

1 _____   6 _____

2 _____   7 _____

3 _____   8 _____

4 _____   9 _____

5 _____   10 _____

Self-Image

Today, I am...

_____

_____

_____

Inspired Action

Today, I take these actions towards my goals...

1 _____   4 _____

2 _____   5 _____

3 _____   6 _____

Sending Love

Today, I send love to these people in my life...

1 _____

2 _____

3 _____

Powerful Positive Affirmation

I HAVE THE POWER TO CREATE CHANGE.

Gratitude

Today, I am so happy and grateful for...

1 _____   6 _____
2 _____   7 _____
3 _____   8 _____
4 _____   9 _____
5 _____   10 _____

Self-Image

Today, I am...

_____

_____

_____

Inspired Action

Today, I take these actions towards my goals...

1 _____   4 _____
2 _____   5 _____
3 _____   6 _____

Sending Love

Today, I send love to these people in my life...

1 _____

2 _____

3 _____

Powerful Positive Affirmation

I BELIEVE IN GOOD THINGS COMING.

Gratitude
Today, I am so happy and grateful for...

1 _____   6 _____
2 _____   7 _____
3 _____   8 _____
4 _____   9 _____
5 _____   10 _____

Self-Image
Today, I am...

_____

_____

_____

Inspired Action
Today, I take these actions towards my goals...

1 _____   4 _____
2 _____   5 _____
3 _____   6 _____

Sending Love
Today, I send love to these people in my life...

1 _____
2 _____
3 _____

Powerful Positive Affirmation

I EXPECT GOOD TO COME TO ME.

Day   Month   Year

Gratitude
Today, I am so happy and grateful for...

1 _____   6 _____
2 _____   7 _____
3 _____   8 _____
4 _____   9 _____
5 _____   10 _____

Self-Image
Today, I am...

_____
_____
_____

Inspired Action
Today, I take these actions towards my goals...

1 _____   4 _____
2 _____   5 _____
3 _____   6 _____

Sending Love
Today, I send love to these people in my life...

1 _____
2 _____
3 _____

Powerful Positive Affirmation

I BELIEVE IN MY UNLIMITED PROSPERITY.

Gratitude

Today, I am so happy and grateful for...

1 _____   6 _____

2 _____   7 _____

3 _____   8 _____

4 _____   9 _____

5 _____   10 _____

Self-Image

Today, I am...

_____

_____

_____

Inspired Action

Today, I take these actions towards my goals...

1 _____   4 _____

2 _____   5 _____

3 _____   6 _____

Sending Love

Today, I send love to these people in my life...

1 _____

2 _____

3 _____

Powerful Positive Affirmation

I CREATE MONEY EASILY AND EFFORTLESSLY.

Gratitude
Today, I am so happy and grateful for...

1 _____
2 _____
3 _____
4 _____
5 _____

6 _____
7 _____
8 _____
9 _____
10 _____

Self-Image
Today, I am...

_____

_____

_____

Inspired Action
Today, I take these actions towards my goals...

1 _____
2 _____
3 _____

4 _____
5 _____
6 _____

Sending Love
Today, I send love to these people in my life...

1 _____
2 _____
3 _____

Powerful Positive Affirmation

I HAVE WEALTH IN EVERY AREA OF MY LIFE.

Gratitude

Today, I am so happy and grateful for...

1 _____   6 _____

2 _____   7 _____

3 _____   8 _____

4 _____   9 _____

5 _____   10 _____

Self-Image

Today, I am...

_____

_____

_____

Inspired Action

Today, I take these actions towards my goals...

1 _____   4 _____

2 _____   5 _____

3 _____   6 _____

Sending Love

Today, I send love to these people in my life...

1 _____

2 _____

3 _____

Powerful Positive Affirmation

I EXPECT ABUNDANCE.

Gratitude

Today, I am so happy and grateful for...

1 _____   6 _____

2 _____   7 _____

3 _____   8 _____

4 _____   9 _____

5 _____   10 _____

Self-Image

Today, I am...

_____

_____

_____

Inspired Action

Today, I take these actions towards my goals...

1 _____   4 _____

2 _____   5 _____

3 _____   6 _____

Sending Love

Today, I send love to these people in my life...

1 _____

2 _____

3 _____

Powerful Positive Affirmation

I AM GRATEFUL FOR ALL THAT I HAVE.

Gratitude
Today, I am so happy and grateful for...

1 _____   6 _____

2 _____   7 _____

3 _____   8 _____

4 _____   9 _____

5 _____   10 _____

Self-Image
Today, I am...

_____

_____

_____

Inspired Action
Today, I take these actions towards my goals...

1 _____   4 _____

2 _____   5 _____

3 _____   6 _____

Sending Love
Today, I send love to these people in my life...

1 _____

2 _____

3 _____

Powerful Positive Affirmation

I HOLD GREAT VISIONS.

Gratitude

Today, I am so happy and grateful for...

1 _____   6 _____
2 _____   7 _____
3 _____   8 _____
4 _____   9 _____
5 _____   10 _____

Self-Image
Today, I am...

_____

_____

_____

Inspired Action
Today, I take these actions towards my goals...

1 _____   4 _____
2 _____   5 _____
3 _____   6 _____

Sending Love
Today, I send love to these people in my life...

1 _____

2 _____

3 _____

Powerful Positive Affirmation

I AM MY OWN BEST FRIEND.

Gratitude

Today, I am so happy and grateful for...

1 _____   6 _____
2 _____   7 _____
3 _____   8 _____
4 _____   9 _____
5 _____   10 _____

Self-Image

Today, I am...

_____

_____

_____

Inspired Action

Today, I take these actions towards my goals...

1 _____   4 _____
2 _____   5 _____
3 _____   6 _____

Sending Love

Today, I send love to these people in my life...

1 _____

2 _____

3 _____

Powerful Positive Affirmation

I KNOW MYSELF BY KNOWING MY VALUES.

Gratitude
Today, I am so happy and grateful for...

1 _____   6 _____
2 _____   7 _____
3 _____   8 _____
4 _____   9 _____
5 _____   10 _____

Self-Image
Today, I am...

_____

_____

_____

Inspired Action
Today, I take these actions towards my goals...

1 _____   4 _____
2 _____   5 _____
3 _____   6 _____

Sending Love
Today, I send love to these people in my life...

1 _____
2 _____
3 _____

Powerful Positive Affirmation

I AM IN ALIGNMENT WITH MY AUTHENTIC SELF.

Gratitude
Today, I am so happy and grateful for...

1 _____   6 _____

2 _____   7 _____

3 _____   8 _____

4 _____   9 _____

5 _____   10 _____

Self-Image
Today, I am...

_____

_____

_____

Inspired Action
Today, I take these actions towards my goals...

1 _____   4 _____

2 _____   5 _____

3 _____   6 _____

Sending Love
Today, I send love to these people in my life...

1 _____

2 _____

3 _____

Powerful Positive Affirmation

I AM CONTINUOUSLY UPGRADING MY SELF-IMAGE TO REFLECT THE PERSON I TRULY WANT TO BE.

Gratitude
Today, I am so happy and grateful for...

1 _____   6 _____
2 _____   7 _____
3 _____   8 _____
4 _____   9 _____
5 _____   10 _____

Self-Image
Today, I am...

_____

_____

_____

Inspired Action
Today, I take these actions towards my goals...

1 _____   4 _____
2 _____   5 _____
3 _____   6 _____

Sending Love
Today, I send love to these people in my life...

1 _____

2 _____

3 _____

Powerful Positive Affirmation

I CONTINUOUSLY STRETCH MYSELF TO CREATE A LIFE THAT IS ABOVE AND BEYOND ANYTHING I HAVE EXPERIENCED IN THE PAST.

Gratitude

Today, I am so happy and grateful for...

1 _____   6 _____

2 _____   7 _____

3 _____   8 _____

4 _____   9 _____

5 _____   10 _____

Self-Image

Today, I am...

_____

_____

_____

Inspired Action

Today, I take these actions towards my goals...

1 _____   4 _____

2 _____   5 _____

3 _____   6 _____

Sending Love

Today, I send love to these people in my life...

1 _____

2 _____

3 _____

Powerful Positive Affirmation

I AM AMAZING! I AM THE PERSON I WANT TO BE.

Gratitude

Today, I am so happy and grateful for...

1 _____   6 _____

2 _____   7 _____

3 _____   8 _____

4 _____   9 _____

5 _____   10 _____

Self-Image

Today, I am...

_____

_____

_____

Inspired Action

Today, I take these actions towards my goals...

1 _____   4 _____

2 _____   5 _____

3 _____   6 _____

Sending Love

Today, I send love to these people in my life...

1 _____

2 _____

3 _____

Powerful Positive Affirmation

MY CAPABILITIES AND POTENTIAL ARE UNLIMITED.

Gratitude

Today, I am so happy and grateful for...

1 _____   6 _____

2 _____   7 _____

3 _____   8 _____

4 _____   9 _____

5 _____   10 _____

Self-Image

Today, I am...

_____

_____

_____

Inspired Action

Today, I take these actions towards my goals...

1 _____   4 _____

2 _____   5 _____

3 _____   6 _____

Sending Love

Today, I send love to these people in my life...

1 _____

2 _____

3 _____

Powerful Positive Affirmation

I AM ALWAYS LEARNING, GROWING AND CHANGING FOR THE BETTER.

Gratitude

Today, I am so happy and grateful for...

1 _____   6 _____

2 _____   7 _____

3 _____   8 _____

4 _____   9 _____

5 _____   10 _____

Self-Image
Today, I am...

_____

_____

_____

Inspired Action
Today, I take these actions towards my goals...

1 _____   4 _____

2 _____   5 _____

3 _____   6 _____

Sending Love
Today, I send love to these people in my life...

1 _____

2 _____

3 _____

Powerful Positive Affirmation

I AM WORTHY OF ALL THE GOOD THINGS IN LIFE.

Gratitude
Today, I am so happy and grateful for...

1 _____   6 _____

2 _____   7 _____

3 _____   8 _____

4 _____   9 _____

5 _____   10 _____

Self-Image
Today, I am...

_____

_____

_____

Inspired Action
Today, I take these actions towards my goals...

1 _____   4 _____

2 _____   5 _____

3 _____   6 _____

Sending Love
Today, I send love to these people in my life...

1 _____

2 _____

3 _____

Powerful Positive Affirmation

I SEE THE GOOD IN ALL THINGS, MYSELF AND OTHERS.

Gratitude

Today, I am so happy and grateful for...

1 _____   6 _____

2 _____   7 _____

3 _____   8 _____

4 _____   9 _____

5 _____   10 _____

Self-Image

Today, I am...

_____

_____

_____

Inspired Action

Today, I take these actions towards my goals...

1 _____   4 _____

2 _____   5 _____

3 _____   6 _____

Sending Love

Today, I send love to these people in my life...

1 _____

2 _____

3 _____

Powerful Positive Affirmation

I LOVE AND TAKE CARE OF MYSELF.

Gratitude
Today, I am so happy and grateful for...

1 _____   6 _____

2 _____   7 _____

3 _____   8 _____

4 _____   9 _____

5 _____   10 _____

Self-Image
Today, I am...

_____

_____

_____

Inspired Action
Today, I take these actions towards my goals...

1 _____   4 _____

2 _____   5 _____

3 _____   6 _____

Sending Love
Today, I send love to these people in my life...

1 _____

2 _____

3 _____

Powerful Positive Affirmation

MY PERSONALITY IS RADIANT WITH CONFIDENCE, CERTAINTY AND OPTIMISM.

Gratitude

Today, I am so happy and grateful for...

1 _____ 6 _____

2 _____ 7 _____

3 _____ 8 _____

4 _____ 9 _____

5 _____ 10 _____

Self-Image
Today, I am...

_____

_____

_____

Inspired Action
Today, I take these actions towards my goals...

1 _____ 4 _____

2 _____ 5 _____

3 _____ 6 _____

Sending Love
Today, I send love to these people in my life...

1 _____

2 _____

3 _____

Powerful Positive Affirmation

I AM CALM AND CONFIDENT.

Gratitude
Today, I am so happy and grateful for...

1 _____   6 _____
2 _____   7 _____
3 _____   8 _____
4 _____   9 _____
5 _____   10 _____

Self-Image
Today, I am...

_____

_____

_____

Inspired Action
Today, I take these actions towards my goals...

1 _____   4 _____
2 _____   5 _____
3 _____   6 _____

Sending Love
Today, I send love to these people in my life...

1 _____

2 _____

3 _____

Powerful Positive Affirmation

I FILL MY MIND WITH HEALTHY, PROSPEROUS AND LOVING THOUGHTS ON A CONTINUOUS BASIS.

Gratitude

Today, I am so happy and grateful for...

1 _____   6 _____

2 _____   7 _____

3 _____   8 _____

4 _____   9 _____

5 _____   10 _____

Self-Image

Today, I am...

_____

_____

_____

Inspired Action

Today, I take these actions towards my goals...

1 _____   4 _____

2 _____   5 _____

3 _____   6 _____

Sending Love

Today, I send love to these people in my life...

1 _____

2 _____

3 _____

Powerful Positive Affirmation

I AM HAPPY AND COMPLETE, TODAY AND FOREVER.

Gratitude

Day   Month   Year

Today, I am so happy and grateful for...

1 _____   6 _____

2 _____   7 _____

3 _____   8 _____

4 _____   9 _____

5 _____   10 _____

Self-Image

Today, I am...

_____

_____

_____

Inspired Action

Today, I take these actions towards my goals...

1 _____   4 _____

2 _____   5 _____

3 _____   6 _____

Sending Love

Today, I send love to these people in my life...

1 _____

2 _____

3 _____

Powerful Positive Affirmation

MY SURROUNDINGS ARE
PEACEFUL AND HARMONIOUS.

Gratitude
Today, I am so happy and grateful for...

1 _____   6 _____
2 _____   7 _____
3 _____   8 _____
4 _____   9 _____
5 _____   10 _____

Self-Image
Today, I am...

_____

_____

_____

Inspired Action
Today, I take these actions towards my goals...

1 _____   4 _____
2 _____   5 _____
3 _____   6 _____

Sending Love
Today, I send love to these people in my life...

1 _____
2 _____
3 _____

Powerful Positive Affirmation

MY LIFE IS FULL OF
LIMITLESS POSSIBILITIES FOR GOOD.

Gratitude
Today, I am so happy and grateful for...

1 _____   6 _____
2 _____   7 _____
3 _____   8 _____
4 _____   9 _____
5 _____   10 _____

Self-Image
Today, I am...

_____
_____
_____

Inspired Action
Today, I take these actions towards my goals...

1 _____   4 _____
2 _____   5 _____
3 _____   6 _____

Sending Love
Today, I send love to these people in my life...

1 _____
2 _____
3 _____

Powerful Positive Affirmation

THERE IS A POWER FOR GOOD IN ME, AND I CAN USE IT!

Gratitude
Today, I am so happy and grateful for...

1 _____ 6 _____

2 _____ 7 _____

3 _____ 8 _____

4 _____ 9 _____

5 _____ 10 _____

Self-Image
Today, I am...

_____

_____

_____

Inspired Action
Today, I take these actions towards my goals...

1 _____ 4 _____

2 _____ 5 _____

3 _____ 6 _____

Sending Love
Today, I send love to these people in my life...

1 _____

2 _____

3 _____

Powerful Positive Affirmation

I EMBODY AND DEMONSTRATE BALANCE AND COMPASSION.

Gratitude
Today, I am so happy and grateful for...

1 _____   6 _____
2 _____   7 _____
3 _____   8 _____
4 _____   9 _____
5 _____   10 _____

Self-Image
Today, I am...

_____

_____

_____

Inspired Action
Today, I take these actions towards my goals...

1 _____   4 _____
2 _____   5 _____
3 _____   6 _____

Sending Love
Today, I send love to these people in my life...

1 _____

2 _____

3 _____

Powerful Positive Affirmation

I AM ENOUGH.

Gratitude

Today, I am so happy and grateful for...

1 _____   6 _____
2 _____   7 _____
3 _____   8 _____
4 _____   9 _____
5 _____   10 _____

Self-Image

Today, I am...

_____

_____

_____

Inspired Action

Today, I take these actions towards my goals...

1 _____   4 _____
2 _____   5 _____
3 _____   6 _____

Sending Love

Today, I send love to these people in my life...

1 _____
2 _____
3 _____

Powerful Positive Affirmation

I AM VALUABLE. I AM A UNIQUE TREASURE.

Gratitude

Today, I am so happy and grateful for...

1 _____   6 _____

2 _____   7 _____

3 _____   8 _____

4 _____   9 _____

5 _____   10 _____

Self-Image

Today, I am...

_____

_____

_____

Inspired Action

Today, I take these actions towards my goals...

1 _____   4 _____

2 _____   5 _____

3 _____   6 _____

Sending Love

Today, I send love to these people in my life...

1 _____

2 _____

3 _____

Powerful Positive Affirmation

I FEEL VALUED AND LOVED.

Gratitude

Today, I am so happy and grateful for...

1 _____   6 _____
2 _____   7 _____
3 _____   8 _____
4 _____   9 _____
5 _____   10 _____

Self-Image

Today, I am...

_____

_____

_____

Inspired Action

Today, I take these actions towards my goals...

1 _____   4 _____
2 _____   5 _____
3 _____   6 _____

Sending Love

Today, I send love to these people in my life...

1 _____

2 _____

3 _____

Powerful Positive Affirmation

I LOVE AND APPRECIATE MYSELF.

Gratitude
Today, I am so happy and grateful for...

1 _____   6 _____
2 _____   7 _____
3 _____   8 _____
4 _____   9 _____
5 _____   10 _____

Self-Image
Today, I am...

_____

_____

_____

Inspired Action
Today, I take these actions towards my goals...

1 _____   4 _____
2 _____   5 _____
3 _____   6 _____

Sending Love
Today, I send love to these people in my life...

1 _____

2 _____

3 _____

Powerful Positive Affirmation

THE UNIVERSE IS FOR ME AND WITH ME.

Gratitude

Today, I am so happy and grateful for...

1 _____
2 _____
3 _____
4 _____
5 _____

6 _____
7 _____
8 _____
9 _____
10 _____

Self-Image

Today, I am...

_____

_____

_____

Inspired Action

Today, I take these actions towards my goals...

1 _____
2 _____
3 _____

4 _____
5 _____
6 _____

Sending Love

Today, I send love to these people in my life...

1 _____
2 _____
3 _____

Powerful Positive Affirmation

THIS IS MY LIFE, AND I CHOOSE
TO ENJOY AND TO PROSPER IN IT.

Gratitude

Today, I am so happy and grateful for...

1 _____   6 _____

2 _____   7 _____

3 _____   8 _____

4 _____   9 _____

5 _____   10 _____

Self-Image

Today, I am...

_____

_____

_____

Inspired Action

Today, I take these actions towards my goals...

1 _____   4 _____

2 _____   5 _____

3 _____   6 _____

Sending Love

Today, I send love to these people in my life...

1 _____

2 _____

3 _____

Powerful Positive Affirmation

I AM A RICH BLESSING TO ALL.

Gratitude

Today, I am so happy and grateful for...

1 _____   6 _____

2 _____   7 _____

3 _____   8 _____

4 _____   9 _____

5 _____   10 _____

Self-Image

Today, I am...

_____

_____

_____

Inspired Action

Today, I take these actions towards my goals...

1 _____   4 _____

2 _____   5 _____

3 _____   6 _____

Sending Love

Today, I send love to these people in my life...

1 _____

2 _____

3 _____

Powerful Positive Affirmation

I DESERVE AND ACCEPT THE BEST.

Gratitude

Today, I am so happy and grateful for...

1 _____   6 _____

2 _____   7 _____

3 _____   8 _____

4 _____   9 _____

5 _____   10 _____

Self-Image

Today, I am...

_____

_____

_____

Inspired Action

Today, I take these actions towards my goals...

1 _____   4 _____

2 _____   5 _____

3 _____   6 _____

Sending Love

Today, I send love to these people in my life...

1 _____

2 _____

3 _____

Powerful Positive Affirmation

I AM BEAUTIFUL, LOVING AND POWERFUL RIGHT NOW.

Gratitude
Today, I am so happy and grateful for...

1 _____   6 _____
2 _____   7 _____
3 _____   8 _____
4 _____   9 _____
5 _____   10 _____

Self-Image
Today, I am...

_____

_____

_____

Inspired Action
Today, I take these actions towards my goals...

1 _____   4 _____
2 _____   5 _____
3 _____   6 _____

Sending Love
Today, I send love to these people in my life...

1 _____
2 _____
3 _____

Powerful Positive Affirmation

I KNOW WHAT TO DO,
HOW TO DO IT,
AND I DO IT BEAUTIFULLY.

Gratitude

Today, I am so happy and grateful for...

1 _____ 6 _____
2 _____ 7 _____
3 _____ 8 _____
4 _____ 9 _____
5 _____ 10 _____

Self-Image

Today, I am...

_____

_____

_____

Inspired Action

Today, I take these actions towards my goals...

1 _____ 4 _____
2 _____ 5 _____
3 _____ 6 _____

Sending Love

Today, I send love to these people in my life...

1 _____

2 _____

3 _____

Powerful Positive Affirmation

I AM THE CONSCIOUSNESS OF SUCCESS ATTRACTING SUCCESS.

Gratitude

Today, I am so happy and grateful for...

1 _____
2 _____
3 _____
4 _____
5 _____

6 _____
7 _____
8 _____
9 _____
10 _____

Self-Image

Today, I am...

_____

_____

_____

Inspired Action

Today, I take these actions towards my goals...

1 _____
2 _____
3 _____

4 _____
5 _____
6 _____

Sending Love

Today, I send love to these people in my life...

1 _____

2 _____

3 _____

Powerful Positive Affirmation

I AM A BLESSING. I AM BLESSED.

Gratitude

Today, I am so happy and grateful for...

1 _____   6 _____

2 _____   7 _____

3 _____   8 _____

4 _____   9 _____

5 _____   10 _____

Self-Image

Today, I am...

_____

_____

_____

Inspired Action

Today, I take these actions towards my goals...

1 _____   4 _____

2 _____   5 _____

3 _____   6 _____

Sending Love

Today, I send love to these people in my life...

1 _____

2 _____

3 _____

Powerful Positive Affirmation

MY PRESENCE IS MY POWER.

Gratitude

Today, I am so happy and grateful for...

1 _____   6 _____

2 _____   7 _____

3 _____   8 _____

4 _____   9 _____

5 _____   10 _____

Self-Image

Today, I am...

_____

_____

_____

Inspired Action

Today, I take these actions towards my goals...

1 _____   4 _____

2 _____   5 _____

3 _____   6 _____

Sending Love

Today, I send love to these people in my life...

1 _____

2 _____

3 _____

Powerful Positive Affirmation

I LOVE MY HIGH-VIBE ENERGY.

Gratitude
Today, I am so happy and grateful for...

1 _____   6 _____
2 _____   7 _____
3 _____   8 _____
4 _____   9 _____
5 _____   10 _____

Self-Image
Today, I am...

_____

_____

_____

Inspired Action
Today, I take these actions towards my goals...

1 _____   4 _____
2 _____   5 _____
3 _____   6 _____

Sending Love
Today, I send love to these people in my life...

1 _____

2 _____

3 _____

Powerful Positive Affirmation

I AM LOVE, LOVED AND LOVING.

Gratitude
Today, I am so happy and grateful for...

1 _____
2 _____
3 _____
4 _____
5 _____

6 _____
7 _____
8 _____
9 _____
10 _____

Self-Image
Today, I am...

_____

_____

_____

Inspired Action
Today, I take these actions towards my goals...

1 _____
2 _____
3 _____

4 _____
5 _____
6 _____

Sending Love
Today, I send love to these people in my life...

1 _____
2 _____
3 _____

Powerful Positive Affirmation

EVERYWHERE I GO,
I ATTRACT LOVE,
PEACE AND HARMONY.

Gratitude
Today, I am so happy and grateful for...

1 _____   6 _____

2 _____   7 _____

3 _____   8 _____

4 _____   9 _____

5 _____   10 _____

Self-Image
Today, I am...

_____

_____

_____

Inspired Action
Today, I take these actions towards my goals...

1 _____   4 _____

2 _____   5 _____

3 _____   6 _____

Sending Love
Today, I send love to these people in my life...

1 _____

2 _____

3 _____

Powerful Positive Affirmation

I SEE EACH DAY AS AN OPPORTUNITY TO SHARE LOVE.

Gratitude
Today, I am so happy and grateful for...

1 _____   6 _____

2 _____   7 _____

3 _____   8 _____

4 _____   9 _____

5 _____   10 _____

Self-Image
Today, I am...

_____

_____

_____

Inspired Action
Today, I take these actions towards my goals...

1 _____   4 _____

2 _____   5 _____

3 _____   6 _____

Sending Love
Today, I send love to these people in my life...

1 _____

2 _____

3 _____

Powerful Positive Affirmation

EVERY CELL OF MY BODY
IS DOING ITS PERFECT WORK.

Gratitude
Today, I am so happy and grateful for...

1 _____
2 _____
3 _____
4 _____
5 _____

6 _____
7 _____
8 _____
9 _____
10 _____

Self-Image
Today, I am...

_____

_____

_____

_____

Inspired Action
Today, I take these actions towards my goals...

1 _____
2 _____
3 _____

4 _____
5 _____
6 _____

Sending Love
Today, I send love to these people in my life...

1 _____

2 _____

3 _____

Powerful Positive Affirmation

I AWAKE EACH MORNING WITH DIVINE ENERGY AND VITALITY.

Gratitude
Today, I am so happy and grateful for...

1 _____
2 _____
3 _____
4 _____
5 _____

6 _____
7 _____
8 _____
9 _____
10 _____

Self-Image
Today, I am...

_____

_____

_____

Inspired Action
Today, I take these actions towards my goals...

1 _____
2 _____
3 _____

4 _____
5 _____
6 _____

Sending Love
Today, I send love to these people in my life...

1 _____
2 _____
3 _____

Powerful Positive Affirmation

I BREATHE DEEPLY, EXERCISE REGULARLY AND FEED ONLY GOOD, NUTRITIOUS FOOD TO MY BODY.

Gratitude

Day   Month   Year

Today, I am so happy and grateful for...

1 _____   6 _____

2 _____   7 _____

3 _____   8 _____

4 _____   9 _____

5 _____   10 _____

Self-Image

Today, I am...

_____

_____

_____

Inspired Action

Today, I take these actions towards my goals...

1 _____   4 _____

2 _____   5 _____

3 _____   6 _____

Sending Love

Today, I send love to these people in my life...

1 _____

2 _____

3 _____

Powerful Positive Affirmation

I EXPECT MY WORK TO ACCOMPLISH ITS PURPOSE.

Gratitude
Today, I am so happy and grateful for...

1 _____   6 _____
2 _____   7 _____
3 _____   8 _____
4 _____   9 _____
5 _____   10 _____

Self-Image
Today, I am...

_____

_____

_____

Inspired Action
Today, I take these actions towards my goals...

1 _____   4 _____
2 _____   5 _____
3 _____   6 _____

Sending Love
Today, I send love to these people in my life...

1 _____
2 _____
3 _____

Powerful Positive Affirmation

I MEET EVERY CHALLENGE AS AN OPPORTUNITY.

Gratitude

Today, I am so happy and grateful for...

1 _____   6 _____

2 _____   7 _____

3 _____   8 _____

4 _____   9 _____

5 _____   10 _____

Self-Image
Today, I am...

_____

_____

_____

Inspired Action
Today, I take these actions towards my goals...

1 _____   4 _____

2 _____   5 _____

3 _____   6 _____

Sending Love
Today, I send love to these people in my life...

1 _____

2 _____

3 _____

Powerful Positive Affirmation

I HAVE PLENTY OF TIME FOR EVERYTHING.

Gratitude

Today, I am so happy and grateful for...

1 _____   6 _____

2 _____   7 _____

3 _____   8 _____

4 _____   9 _____

5 _____   10 _____

Self-Image
Today, I am...

_____

_____

_____

Inspired Action
Today, I take these actions towards my goals...

1 _____   4 _____

2 _____   5 _____

3 _____   6 _____

Sending Love
Today, I send love to these people in my life...

1 _____

2 _____

3 _____

Powerful Positive Affirmation

I DESERVE AND EXPECT THE BEST.

Gratitude

Today, I am so happy and grateful for...

1 _____   6 _____
2 _____   7 _____
3 _____   8 _____
4 _____   9 _____
5 _____   10 _____

Self-Image

Today, I am...

_____

_____

_____

Inspired Action

Today, I take these actions towards my goals...

1 _____   4 _____
2 _____   5 _____
3 _____   6 _____

Sending Love

Today, I send love to these people in my life...

1 _____

2 _____

3 _____

Powerful Positive Affirmation

LIFE LOVES ME!

Gratitude
Today, I am so happy and grateful for...

1 _____   6 _____
2 _____   7 _____
3 _____   8 _____
4 _____   9 _____
5 _____   10 _____

Self-Image
Today, I am...

_____

_____

_____

Inspired Action
Today, I take these actions towards my goals...

1 _____   4 _____
2 _____   5 _____
3 _____   6 _____

Sending Love
Today, I send love to these people in my life...

1 _____
2 _____
3 _____

Powerful Positive Affirmation

I ALWAYS FEEL GOOD. AS A RESULT, MY BODY FEELS GOOD, AND I RADIATE GOOD FEELINGS.

Gratitude

Today, I am so happy and grateful for...

1 _____   6 _____

2 _____   7 _____

3 _____   8 _____

4 _____   9 _____

5 _____   10 _____

Self-Image
Today, I am...

_____

_____

_____

Inspired Action
Today, I take these actions towards my goals...

1 _____   4 _____

2 _____   5 _____

3 _____   6 _____

Sending Love
Today, I send love to these people in my life...

1 _____

2 _____

3 _____

Powerful Positive Affirmation

I ALLOW GOOD TO FLOW TO ME.

Gratitude
Today, I am so happy and grateful for...

1 _____   6 _____
2 _____   7 _____
3 _____   8 _____
4 _____   9 _____
5 _____   10 _____

Self-Image
Today, I am...

_____

_____

_____

Inspired Action
Today, I take these actions towards my goals...

1 _____   4 _____
2 _____   5 _____
3 _____   6 _____

Sending Love
Today, I send love to these people in my life...

1 _____
2 _____
3 _____

Powerful Positive Affirmation

I AM STRONG AND CONFIDENT.

Gratitude

Today, I am so happy and grateful for...

1 _____   6 _____
2 _____   7 _____
3 _____   8 _____
4 _____   9 _____
5 _____   10 _____

Self-Image

Today, I am...

_____

_____

_____

Inspired Action

Today, I take these actions towards my goals...

1 _____   4 _____
2 _____   5 _____
3 _____   6 _____

Sending Love

Today, I send love to these people in my life...

1 _____
2 _____
3 _____

Powerful Positive Affirmation

ABUNDANCE FLOWS THROUGH MY OPEN ARMS.

Gratitude

Today, I am so happy and grateful for...

1 _____ 6 _____

2 _____ 7 _____

3 _____ 8 _____

4 _____ 9 _____

5 _____ 10 _____

Self-Image

Today, I am...

_____

_____

_____

Inspired Action

Today, I take these actions towards my goals...

1 _____ 4 _____

2 _____ 5 _____

3 _____ 6 _____

Sending Love

Today, I send love to these people in my life...

1 _____

2 _____

3 _____

Powerful Positive Affirmation

I AM CONNECTED TO THE ABUNDANCE OF THE UNIVERSE.

Gratitude
Today, I am so happy and grateful for...

1 _____   6 _____

2 _____   7 _____

3 _____   8 _____

4 _____   9 _____

5 _____   10 _____

Self-Image
Today, I am...

_____

_____

_____

Inspired Action
Today, I take these actions towards my goals...

1 _____   4 _____

2 _____   5 _____

3 _____   6 _____

Sending Love
Today, I send love to these people in my life...

1 _____

2 _____

3 _____

Powerful Positive Affirmation

I AM FINANCIALLY FREE.

Gratitude
Today, I am so happy and grateful for...

1 _____   6 _____
2 _____   7 _____
3 _____   8 _____
4 _____   9 _____
5 _____   10 _____

Self-Image
Today, I am...

_____

_____

_____

Inspired Action
Today, I take these actions towards my goals...

1 _____   4 _____
2 _____   5 _____
3 _____   6 _____

Sending Love
Today, I send love to these people in my life...

1 _____
2 _____
3 _____

Powerful Positive Affirmation

I AM GRATEFUL FOR THE RICHES IN MY LIFE.

Gratitude

Today, I am so happy and grateful for...

1 _____   6 _____

2 _____   7 _____

3 _____   8 _____

4 _____   9 _____

5 _____   10 _____

Self-Image

Today, I am...

_____

_____

_____

Inspired Action

Today, I take these actions towards my goals...

1 _____   4 _____

2 _____   5 _____

3 _____   6 _____

Sending Love

Today, I send love to these people in my life...

1 _____

2 _____

3 _____

Powerful Positive Affirmation

I AM WEALTHIER EACH DAY IN EVERY WAY.

Gratitude
Today, I am so happy and grateful for...

1 _____   6 _____
2 _____   7 _____
3 _____   8 _____
4 _____   9 _____
5 _____   10 _____

Self-Image
Today, I am...

_____

_____

_____

Inspired Action
Today, I take these actions towards my goals...

1 _____   4 _____
2 _____   5 _____
3 _____   6 _____

Sending Love
Today, I send love to these people in my life...

1 _____
2 _____
3 _____

Powerful Positive Affirmation

I AM RESPECTED BY EVERYONE IN MY WORK ENVIRONMENT.

Gratitude
Today, I am so happy and grateful for...

1 _____   6 _____
2 _____   7 _____
3 _____   8 _____
4 _____   9 _____
5 _____   10 _____

Self-Image
Today, I am...

_____
_____
_____

Inspired Action
Today, I take these actions towards my goals...

1 _____   4 _____
2 _____   5 _____
3 _____   6 _____

Sending Love
Today, I send love to these people in my life...

1 _____
2 _____
3 _____

Powerful Positive Affirmation

I EXPECT THE BEST,
AND THE BEST ALWAYS HAPPENS.

Gratitude
Today, I am so happy and grateful for...

1 _____   6 _____
2 _____   7 _____
3 _____   8 _____
4 _____   9 _____
5 _____   10 _____

Self-Image
Today, I am...

_____

_____

_____

Inspired Action
Today, I take these actions towards my goals...

1 _____   4 _____
2 _____   5 _____
3 _____   6 _____

Sending Love
Today, I send love to these people in my life...

1 _____
2 _____
3 _____

Powerful Positive Affirmation

I AM OPEN AND RECEPTIVE TO GREATER GOOD AND GREATER UNDERSTANDING.

Gratitude

Today, I am so happy and grateful for...

1 _____   6 _____
2 _____   7 _____
3 _____   8 _____
4 _____   9 _____
5 _____   10 _____

Self-Image

Today, I am...

_____

_____

_____

Inspired Action

Today, I take these actions towards my goals...

1 _____   4 _____
2 _____   5 _____
3 _____   6 _____

Sending Love

Today, I send love to these people in my life...

1 _____

2 _____

3 _____

Powerful Positive Affirmation

THE UNIVERSE IS ALWAYS SAYING "YES!"

Gratitude
Today, I am so happy and grateful for...

1 _____ 6 _____
2 _____ 7 _____
3 _____ 8 _____
4 _____ 9 _____
5 _____ 10 _____

Self-Image
Today, I am...

_____
_____
_____

Inspired Action
Today, I take these actions towards my goals...

1 _____ 4 _____
2 _____ 5 _____
3 _____ 6 _____

Sending Love
Today, I send love to these people in my life...

1 _____
2 _____
3 _____

Powerful Positive Affirmation

I SEE EACH DAY AS AN OPPORTUNITY TO SHARE LOVE.

Gratitude
Today, I am so happy and grateful for...

1 _____   6 _____
2 _____   7 _____
3 _____   8 _____
4 _____   9 _____
5 _____   10 _____

Self-Image
Today, I am...

_____
_____
_____

Inspired Action
Today, I take these actions towards my goals...

1 _____   4 _____
2 _____   5 _____
3 _____   6 _____

Sending Love
Today, I send love to these people in my life...

1 _____
2 _____
3 _____

Powerful Positive Affirmation

I LET GO OF ALL THAT DOESN'T SERVE ME.

Gratitude
Today, I am so happy and grateful for...

1 _____   6 _____

2 _____   7 _____

3 _____   8 _____

4 _____   9 _____

5 _____   10 _____

Self-Image
Today, I am...

_____

_____

_____

Inspired Action
Today, I take these actions towards my goals...

1 _____   4 _____

2 _____   5 _____

3 _____   6 _____

Sending Love
Today, I send love to these people in my life...

1 _____

2 _____

3 _____

Powerful Positive Affirmation

I ONLY THINK ABOUT THE GOOD THAT I DESIRE.

Gratitude
Today, I am so happy and grateful for...

1 _____   6 _____
2 _____   7 _____
3 _____   8 _____
4 _____   9 _____
5 _____   10 _____

Self-Image
Today, I am...

_____

_____

_____

Inspired Action
Today, I take these actions towards my goals...

1 _____   4 _____
2 _____   5 _____
3 _____   6 _____

Sending Love
Today, I send love to these people in my life...

1 _____
2 _____
3 _____

Powerful Positive Affirmation

IT'S ALL WORKING OUT FOR ME.
IT ALWAYS WORKS OUT FOR ME.

Gratitude
Today, I am so happy and grateful for...

1 _____   6 _____
2 _____   7 _____
3 _____   8 _____
4 _____   9 _____
5 _____   10 _____

Self-Image
Today, I am...

_____

_____

_____

Inspired Action
Today, I take these actions towards my goals...

1 _____   4 _____
2 _____   5 _____
3 _____   6 _____

Sending Love
Today, I send love to these people in my life...

1 _____
2 _____
3 _____

Powerful Positive Affirmation

I LOVE AND CARE FOR MYSELF.

Gratitude

Today, I am so happy and grateful for...

1 _____
2 _____
3 _____
4 _____
5 _____

6 _____
7 _____
8 _____
9 _____
10 _____

Self-Image
Today, I am...

_____

_____

_____

Inspired Action
Today, I take these actions towards my goals...

1 _____
2 _____
3 _____

4 _____
5 _____
6 _____

Sending Love
Today, I send love to these people in my life...

1 _____
2 _____
3 _____

Powerful Positive Affirmation

ABUNDANCE IS EVERYWHERE.

Gratitude
Today, I am so happy and grateful for...

1 _____   6 _____

2 _____   7 _____

3 _____   8 _____

4 _____   9 _____

5 _____   10 _____

Self-Image
Today, I am...

_____

_____

_____

Inspired Action
Today, I take these actions towards my goals...

1 _____   4 _____

2 _____   5 _____

3 _____   6 _____

Sending Love
Today, I send love to these people in my life...

1 _____

2 _____

3 _____

Powerful Positive Affirmation

I AM AN ABUNDANCE MAGNET.

Gratitude

Today, I am so happy and grateful for...

1 _____   6 _____

2 _____   7 _____

3 _____   8 _____

4 _____   9 _____

5 _____   10 _____

Self-Image

Today, I am...

_____

_____

_____

Inspired Action

Today, I take these actions towards my goals...

1 _____   4 _____

2 _____   5 _____

3 _____   6 _____

Sending Love

Today, I send love to these people in my life...

1 _____

2 _____

3 _____

Powerful Positive Affirmation

I AM LOVE.

Gratitude
Today, I am so happy and grateful for...

1 _____ 6 _____

2 _____ 7 _____

3 _____ 8 _____

4 _____ 9 _____

5 _____ 10 _____

Self-Image
Today, I am...

_____

_____

_____

Inspired Action
Today, I take these actions towards my goals...

1 _____ 4 _____

2 _____ 5 _____

3 _____ 6 _____

Sending Love
Today, I send love to these people in my life...

1 _____

2 _____

3 _____

Powerful Positive Affirmation

I GIVE THANKS FOR A CLEAR AND DECISIVE MIND THAT THINKS HEALTHY AND CONSTRUCTIVE THOUGHTS.

Gratitude

Today, I am so happy and grateful for...

1 _____   6 _____
2 _____   7 _____
3 _____   8 _____
4 _____   9 _____
5 _____   10 _____

Self-Image

Today, I am...

_____

_____

_____

Inspired Action

Today, I take these actions towards my goals...

1 _____   4 _____
2 _____   5 _____
3 _____   6 _____

Sending Love

Today, I send love to these people in my life...

1 _____

2 _____

3 _____

Powerful Positive Affirmation

MY THANKFUL HEART ATTRACTS LOVING PEOPLE WHO ARE THOUGHTFUL, GENTLE AND KIND.

Gratitude

Today, I am so happy and grateful for...

1 _____   6 _____

2 _____   7 _____

3 _____   8 _____

4 _____   9 _____

5 _____   10 _____

Self-Image

Today, I am...

_____

_____

_____

Inspired Action

Today, I take these actions towards my goals...

1 _____   4 _____

2 _____   5 _____

3 _____   6 _____

Sending Love

Today, I send love to these people in my life...

1 _____

2 _____

3 _____

Powerful Positive Affirmation

THE MORE GOOD I AM GRATEFUL FOR
THE MORE GOOD I EXPERIENCE.

Gratitude
Today, I am so happy and grateful for...

1 _____   6 _____

2 _____   7 _____

3 _____   8 _____

4 _____   9 _____

5 _____   10 _____

Self-Image
Today, I am...

_____

_____

_____

Inspired Action
Today, I take these actions towards my goals...

1 _____   4 _____

2 _____   5 _____

3 _____   6 _____

Sending Love
Today, I send love to these people in my life...

1 _____

2 _____

3 _____

Powerful Positive Affirmation

I APPRECIATE MY LIFE.

Gratitude
Today, I am so happy and grateful for...

1 _____   6 _____
2 _____   7 _____
3 _____   8 _____
4 _____   9 _____
5 _____   10 _____

Self-Image
Today, I am...

_____
_____
_____

Inspired Action
Today, I take these actions towards my goals...

1 _____   4 _____
2 _____   5 _____
3 _____   6 _____

Sending Love
Today, I send love to these people in my life...

1 _____
2 _____
3 _____

Powerful Positive Affirmation

I APPRECIATE MY SELF-HEALING POWER.

Gratitude
Today, I am so happy and grateful for...

1 _____   6 _____

2 _____   7 _____

3 _____   8 _____

4 _____   9 _____

5 _____   10 _____

Self-Image
Today, I am...

_____

_____

_____

Inspired Action
Today, I take these actions towards my goals...

1 _____   4 _____

2 _____   5 _____

3 _____   6 _____

Sending Love
Today, I send love to these people in my life...

1 _____

2 _____

3 _____

Powerful Positive Affirmation

I AM GRATEFUL FOR MY INTUITIVE ABILITY TO ATTRACT HEALTHY, LOVING AND HARMONIOUS RELATIONSHIPS.

Gratitude
Today, I am so happy and grateful for...

1 _____   6 _____
2 _____   7 _____
3 _____   8 _____
4 _____   9 _____
5 _____   10 _____

Self-Image
Today, I am...

_____

_____

_____

Inspired Action
Today, I take these actions towards my goals...

1 _____   4 _____
2 _____   5 _____
3 _____   6 _____

Sending Love
Today, I send love to these people in my life...

1 _____
2 _____
3 _____

Powerful Positive Affirmation

I DELIGHT IN THE GRACE AND GLORY OF MY SPIRITUAL JOURNEY THAT MAKES THE WAY CLEAR AND SAFE FOR ME.

Gratitude
Today, I am so happy and grateful for...

1 _____   6 _____

2 _____   7 _____

3 _____   8 _____

4 _____   9 _____

5 _____   10 _____

Self-Image
Today, I am...

_____

_____

_____

Inspired Action
Today, I take these actions towards my goals...

1 _____   4 _____

2 _____   5 _____

3 _____   6 _____

Sending Love
Today, I send love to these people in my life...

1 _____

2 _____

3 _____

Powerful Positive Affirmation

WHEREVER I GO AND WHATEVER I DO, I AM ALWAYS MET WITH LOVE AND APPRECIATION.

Gratitude

Today, I am so happy and grateful for...

1 _____   6 _____
2 _____   7 _____
3 _____   8 _____
4 _____   9 _____
5 _____   10 _____

Self-Image

Today, I am...

_____

_____

_____

Inspired Action

Today, I take these actions towards my goals...

1 _____   4 _____
2 _____   5 _____
3 _____   6 _____

Sending Love

Today, I send love to these people in my life...

1 _____
2 _____
3 _____

Powerful Positive Affirmation

I AM BLESSED TO BE OF SERVICE
AND AM GRATEFUL FOR THE OPPORTUNITY
TO MAKE A DIFFERENCE IN THE WORLD.

Gratitude

Today, I am so happy and grateful for...

1 _____   6 _____

2 _____   7 _____

3 _____   8 _____

4 _____   9 _____

5 _____   10 _____

Self-Image

Today, I am...

_____

_____

_____

Inspired Action

Today, I take these actions towards my goals...

1 _____   4 _____

2 _____   5 _____

3 _____   6 _____

Sending Love

Today, I send love to these people in my life...

1 _____

2 _____

3 _____

Powerful Positive Affirmation

I AM GRATEFUL FOR AN ABUNDANCE OF LOVE, HEALTH, WEALTH AND HAPPINESS.

Gratitude
Today, I am so happy and grateful for...

1 _____ 6 _____

2 _____ 7 _____

3 _____ 8 _____

4 _____ 9 _____

5 _____ 10 _____

Self-Image
Today, I am...

_____

_____

_____

Inspired Action
Today, I take these actions towards my goals...

1 _____ 4 _____

2 _____ 5 _____

3 _____ 6 _____

Sending Love
Today, I send love to these people in my life...

1 _____

2 _____

3 _____

Powerful Positive Affirmation

I AM GRATEFUL FOR THE DIVINE PROCESS
THAT KNOWS ONLY LIMITLESS POSSIBILITIES.

Gratitude

Today, I am so happy and grateful for...

1 _____
2 _____
3 _____
4 _____
5 _____

6 _____
7 _____
8 _____
9 _____
10 _____

Self-Image

Today, I am...

_____

_____

_____

Inspired Action

Today, I take these actions towards my goals...

1 _____
2 _____
3 _____

4 _____
5 _____
6 _____

Sending Love

Today, I send love to these people in my life...

1 _____

2 _____

3 _____

Powerful Positive Affirmation

I AM GRATEFUL FOR THE OPPORTUNITIES THAT TURN INTO LIMITLESS POSSIBILITIES FOR ME.

Gratitude
Today, I am so happy and grateful for...

1 _____   6 _____

2 _____   7 _____

3 _____   8 _____

4 _____   9 _____

5 _____   10 _____

Self-Image
Today, I am...

_____

_____

_____

Inspired Action
Today, I take these actions towards my goals...

1 _____   4 _____

2 _____   5 _____

3 _____   6 _____

Sending Love
Today, I send love to these people in my life...

1 _____

2 _____

3 _____

Powerful Positive Affirmation

I AM GRATEFUL FOR THE LOVE I FEEL IN MY HEART.

Gratitude
Today, I am so happy and grateful for...

1 _____ 6 _____
2 _____ 7 _____
3 _____ 8 _____
4 _____ 9 _____
5 _____ 10 _____

Self-Image
Today, I am...

_____
_____
_____

Inspired Action
Today, I take these actions towards my goals...

1 _____ 4 _____
2 _____ 5 _____
3 _____ 6 _____

Sending Love
Today, I send love to these people in my life...

1 _____
2 _____
3 _____

Powerful Positive Affirmation

I AM SUCCESSFUL AND BRIGHT!

Gratitude

Today, I am so happy and grateful for...

1 _____   6 _____

2 _____   7 _____

3 _____   8 _____

4 _____   9 _____

5 _____   10 _____

Self-Image

Today, I am...

_____

_____

_____

Inspired Action

Today, I take these actions towards my goals...

1 _____   4 _____

2 _____   5 _____

3 _____   6 _____

Sending Love

Today, I send love to these people in my life...

1 _____

2 _____

3 _____

Powerful Positive Affirmation

I REACH FOR THE BEST FEELING THOUGHTS MOMENT BY MOMENT.

Gratitude
Today, I am so happy and grateful for...

1 _____
2 _____
3 _____
4 _____
5 _____

6 _____
7 _____
8 _____
9 _____
10 _____

Self-Image
Today, I am...

_____
_____
_____

Inspired Action
Today, I take these actions towards my goals...

1 _____
2 _____
3 _____

4 _____
5 _____
6 _____

Sending Love
Today, I send love to these people in my life...

1 _____
2 _____
3 _____

Powerful Positive Affirmation

I AM CONFIDENT AND STRONG.

Gratitude
Today, I am so happy and grateful for...

1 _____   6 _____
2 _____   7 _____
3 _____   8 _____
4 _____   9 _____
5 _____   10 _____

Self-Image
Today, I am...

_____
_____
_____

Inspired Action
Today, I take these actions towards my goals...

1 _____   4 _____
2 _____   5 _____
3 _____   6 _____

Sending Love
Today, I send love to these people in my life...

1 _____
2 _____
3 _____

Powerful Positive Affirmation

I CHOOSE LOVE, INSPIRATION AND HAPPINESS.

Gratitude

Today, I am so happy and grateful for...

1 _____   6 _____
2 _____   7 _____
3 _____   8 _____
4 _____   9 _____
5 _____   10 _____

Self-Image

Today, I am...

_____

_____

_____

Inspired Action

Today, I take these actions towards my goals...

1 _____   4 _____
2 _____   5 _____
3 _____   6 _____

Sending Love

Today, I send love to these people in my life...

1 _____

2 _____

3 _____

Powerful Positive Affirmation

I AM POWERFUL, AND I CAN FEEL MY POWER.

Gratitude

Today, I am so happy and grateful for...

1 _____
2 _____
3 _____
4 _____
5 _____

6 _____
7 _____
8 _____
9 _____
10 _____

Self-Image

Today, I am...

_____

_____

_____

Inspired Action

Today, I take these actions towards my goals...

1 _____
2 _____
3 _____

4 _____
5 _____
6 _____

Sending Love

Today, I send love to these people in my life...

1 _____
2 _____
3 _____

Powerful Positive Affirmation

EVERY DAY, IN EVERY WAY,
I AM GETTING HEALTHIER AND HEALTHIER
AND FEELING BETTER AND BETTER.

Gratitude
Today, I am so happy and grateful for...

1 _____   6 _____
2 _____   7 _____
3 _____   8 _____
4 _____   9 _____
5 _____   10 _____

Self-Image
Today, I am...

_____

_____

_____

Inspired Action
Today, I take these actions towards my goals...

1 _____   4 _____
2 _____   5 _____
3 _____   6 _____

Sending Love
Today, I send love to these people in my life...

1 _____
2 _____
3 _____

Powerful Positive Affirmation

I LOVE MYSELF AND I AM PERFECTLY HEALTHY.

Gratitude

Today, I am so happy and grateful for...

1 _____   6 _____

2 _____   7 _____

3 _____   8 _____

4 _____   9 _____

5 _____   10 _____

Self-Image

Today, I am...

_____

_____

_____

Inspired Action

Today, I take these actions towards my goals...

1 _____   4 _____

2 _____   5 _____

3 _____   6 _____

Sending Love

Today, I send love to these people in my life...

1 _____

2 _____

3 _____

Powerful Positive Affirmation

EVERY CELL IN MY BODY IS
HEALTH-CONSCIOUS AND VIBRANT.

Gratitude
Today, I am so happy and grateful for...

1 _____   6 _____

2 _____   7 _____

3 _____   8 _____

4 _____   9 _____

5 _____   10 _____

Self-Image
Today, I am...

_____

_____

_____

Inspired Action
Today, I take these actions towards my goals...

1 _____   4 _____

2 _____   5 _____

3 _____   6 _____

Sending Love
Today, I send love to these people in my life...

1 _____

2 _____

3 _____

Powerful Positive Affirmation

I AM FULL OF ENERGY AND VITALITY, AND MY MIND IS CALM AND PEACEFUL.

Gratitude
Today, I am so happy and grateful for...

1 _____   6 _____

2 _____   7 _____

3 _____   8 _____

4 _____   9 _____

5 _____   10 _____

Self-Image
Today, I am...

_____

_____

_____

Inspired Action
Today, I take these actions towards my goals...

1 _____   4 _____

2 _____   5 _____

3 _____   6 _____

Sending Love
Today, I send love to these people in my life...

1 _____

2 _____

3 _____

Powerful Positive Affirmation

I THINK ONLY POSITIVE THOUGHTS AND AM ALWAYS HAPPY AND JOYOUS, NO MATTER WHAT THE EXTERNAL CONDITIONS ARE.

Gratitude

Today, I am so happy and grateful for...

1 _____   6 _____

2 _____   7 _____

3 _____   8 _____

4 _____   9 _____

5 _____   10 _____

Self-Image

Today, I am...

_____

_____

_____

Inspired Action

Today, I take these actions towards my goals...

1 _____   4 _____

2 _____   5 _____

3 _____   6 _____

Sending Love

Today, I send love to these people in my life...

1 _____

2 _____

3 _____

Powerful Positive Affirmation

EVERY DAY IS A NEW DAY FULL OF HOPE, HAPPINESS, AND HEALTH.

Gratitude
Today, I am so happy and grateful for...

1 _____
2 _____
3 _____
4 _____
5 _____

6 _____
7 _____
8 _____
9 _____
10 _____

Self-Image
Today, I am...

_____

_____

_____

Inspired Action
Today, I take these actions towards my goals...

1 _____
2 _____
3 _____

4 _____
5 _____
6 _____

Sending Love
Today, I send love to these people in my life...

1 _____
2 _____
3 _____

Powerful Positive Affirmation

IT IS SAFE FOR ME TO BE VULNERABLE.

Gratitude

Today, I am so happy and grateful for...

1 _____   6 _____

2 _____   7 _____

3 _____   8 _____

4 _____   9 _____

5 _____   10 _____

Self-Image
Today, I am...

_____

_____

_____

Inspired Action
Today, I take these actions towards my goals...

1 _____   4 _____

2 _____   5 _____

3 _____   6 _____

Sending Love
Today, I send love to these people in my life...

1 _____

2 _____

3 _____

Powerful Positive Affirmation

I MAKE DECISIONS FROM MY TRUE INNER SELF.

Gratitude
Today, I am so happy and grateful for...

1 _____   6 _____
2 _____   7 _____
3 _____   8 _____
4 _____   9 _____
5 _____   10 _____

Self-Image
Today, I am...

_____

_____

_____

Inspired Action
Today, I take these actions towards my goals...

1 _____   4 _____
2 _____   5 _____
3 _____   6 _____

Sending Love
Today, I send love to these people in my life...

1 _____
2 _____
3 _____

Powerful Positive Affirmation

I AM GETTING BETTER AND BETTER EVERY DAY.

Gratitude
Today, I am so happy and grateful for...

1 _____
2 _____
3 _____
4 _____
5 _____

6 _____
7 _____
8 _____
9 _____
10 _____

Self-Image
Today, I am...

_____

_____

_____

Inspired Action
Today, I take these actions towards my goals...

1 _____
2 _____
3 _____

4 _____
5 _____
6 _____

Sending Love
Today, I send love to these people in my life...

1 _____
2 _____
3 _____

Powerful Positive Affirmation

ALL I NEED IS WITHIN ME RIGHT NOW.

Gratitude
Today, I am so happy and grateful for...

1 _____   6 _____
2 _____   7 _____
3 _____   8 _____
4 _____   9 _____
5 _____   10 _____

Self-Image
Today, I am...

_____

_____

_____

Inspired Action
Today, I take these actions towards my goals...

1 _____   4 _____
2 _____   5 _____
3 _____   6 _____

Sending Love
Today, I send love to these people in my life...

1 _____
2 _____
3 _____

Powerful Positive Affirmation

I WAKE UP INSPIRED TO CREATE THE DAY AHEAD.

Gratitude

Today, I am so happy and grateful for...

1 _____   6 _____

2 _____   7 _____

3 _____   8 _____

4 _____   9 _____

5 _____   10 _____

Self-Image

Today, I am...

_____

_____

_____

Inspired Action

Today, I take these actions towards my goals...

1 _____   4 _____

2 _____   5 _____

3 _____   6 _____

Sending Love

Today, I send love to these people in my life...

1 _____

2 _____

3 _____

Powerful Positive Affirmation

I LOVE AND APPROVE OF MYSELF.

Gratitude
Today, I am so happy and grateful for...

1 _____
2 _____
3 _____
4 _____
5 _____

6 _____
7 _____
8 _____
9 _____
10 _____

Self-Image
Today, I am...

_____

_____

_____

Inspired Action
Today, I take these actions towards my goals...

1 _____
2 _____
3 _____

4 _____
5 _____
6 _____

Sending Love
Today, I send love to these people in my life...

1 _____
2 _____
3 _____

Powerful Positive Affirmation

I LOVE WHO I AM. I LOVE WHO I HAVE BECOME.

Gratitude

Today, I am so happy and grateful for...

1 _____   6 _____
2 _____   7 _____
3 _____   8 _____
4 _____   9 _____
5 _____   10 _____

Self-Image

Today, I am...

_____
_____
_____
_____

Inspired Action

Today, I take these actions towards my goals...

1 _____   4 _____
2 _____   5 _____
3 _____   6 _____

Sending Love

Today, I send love to these people in my life...

1 _____
2 _____
3 _____

Powerful Positive Affirmation

I AM AN UNSTOPPABLE FORCE OF NATURE.

Gratitude
Today, I am so happy and grateful for...

1 _____   6 _____

2 _____   7 _____

3 _____   8 _____

4 _____   9 _____

5 _____   10 _____

Self-Image
Today, I am...

_____

_____

_____

Inspired Action
Today, I take these actions towards my goals...

1 _____   4 _____

2 _____   5 _____

3 _____   6 _____

Sending Love
Today, I send love to these people in my life...

1 _____

2 _____

3 _____

Powerful Positive Affirmation

I AM A LIVING, BREATHING EXAMPLE OF MOTIVATION.

Gratitude
Today, I am so happy and grateful for...

1 _____   6 _____

2 _____   7 _____

3 _____   8 _____

4 _____   9 _____

5 _____   10 _____

Self-Image
Today, I am...

_____

_____

_____

Inspired Action
Today, I take these actions towards my goals...

1 _____   4 _____

2 _____   5 _____

3 _____   6 _____

Sending Love
Today, I send love to these people in my life...

1 _____

2 _____

3 _____

Powerful Positive Affirmation

I AM LIVING WITH ABUNDANCE AND JOY.

Gratitude

Today, I am so happy and grateful for...

1 _____   6 _____

2 _____   7 _____

3 _____   8 _____

4 _____   9 _____

5 _____   10 _____

Self-Image

Today, I am...

_____

_____

_____

Inspired Action

Today, I take these actions towards my goals...

1 _____   4 _____

2 _____   5 _____

3 _____   6 _____

Sending Love

Today, I send love to these people in my life...

1 _____

2 _____

3 _____

Powerful Positive Affirmation

I AM HAVING A POSITIVE AND INSPIRING IMPACT ON THE PEOPLE I COME INTO CONTACT WITH.

Gratitude

Today, I am so happy and grateful for...

1 _____   6 _____

2 _____   7 _____

3 _____   8 _____

4 _____   9 _____

5 _____   10 _____

Self-Image

Today, I am...

_____

_____

_____

Inspired Action

Today, I take these actions towards my goals...

1 _____   4 _____

2 _____   5 _____

3 _____   6 _____

Sending Love

Today, I send love to these people in my life...

1 _____

2 _____

3 _____

Powerful Positive Affirmation

I AM INSPIRING PEOPLE THROUGH MY WORK.

Gratitude

Today, I am so happy and grateful for...

1 _____   6 _____

2 _____   7 _____

3 _____   8 _____

4 _____   9 _____

5 _____   10 _____

Self-Image

Today, I am...

_____

_____

_____

Inspired Action

Today, I take these actions towards my goals...

1 _____   4 _____

2 _____   5 _____

3 _____   6 _____

Sending Love

Today, I send love to these people in my life...

1 _____

2 _____

3 _____

Powerful Positive Affirmation

TODAY IS A PHENOMENAL DAY.

Gratitude

Today, I am so happy and grateful for...

1 _____   6 _____
2 _____   7 _____
3 _____   8 _____
4 _____   9 _____
5 _____   10 _____

Self-Image

Today, I am...

_____
_____
_____

Inspired Action

Today, I take these actions towards my goals...

1 _____   4 _____
2 _____   5 _____
3 _____   6 _____

Sending Love

Today, I send love to these people in my life...

1 _____
2 _____
3 _____

Powerful Positive Affirmation

I AM TURNING UP THE
VOLUME OF POSITIVITY IN MY LIFE.

Gratitude
Today, I am so happy and grateful for...

1 _____   6 _____

2 _____   7 _____

3 _____   8 _____

4 _____   9 _____

5 _____   10 _____

Self-Image
Today, I am...

_____

_____

_____

Inspired Action
Today, I take these actions towards my goals...

1 _____   4 _____

2 _____   5 _____

3 _____   6 _____

Sending Love
Today, I send love to these people in my life...

1 _____

2 _____

3 _____

Powerful Positive Affirmation

I AM FILLED WITH FOCUS.

Gratitude

Today, I am so happy and grateful for...

1 _____   6 _____

2 _____   7 _____

3 _____   8 _____

4 _____   9 _____

5 _____   10 _____

Self-Image

Today, I am...

_____

_____

_____

Inspired Action

Today, I take these actions towards my goals...

1 _____   4 _____

2 _____   5 _____

3 _____   6 _____

Sending Love

Today, I send love to these people in my life...

1 _____

2 _____

3 _____

Powerful Positive Affirmation

I AM LED BY MY DREAMS.

Gratitude
Today, I am so happy and grateful for...

1 _____ 6 _____

2 _____ 7 _____

3 _____ 8 _____

4 _____ 9 _____

5 _____ 10 _____

Self-Image
Today, I am...

_____

_____

_____

Inspired Action
Today, I take these actions towards my goals...

1 _____ 4 _____

2 _____ 5 _____

3 _____ 6 _____

Sending Love
Today, I send love to these people in my life...

1 _____

2 _____

3 _____

Powerful Positive Affirmation

I AM INDEPENDENT AND SELF-SUFFICIENT.

Gratitude

Today, I am so happy and grateful for...

1 _____   6 _____
2 _____   7 _____
3 _____   8 _____
4 _____   9 _____
5 _____   10 _____

Self-Image

Today, I am...

_____

_____

_____

Inspired Action

Today, I take these actions towards my goals...

1 _____   4 _____
2 _____   5 _____
3 _____   6 _____

Sending Love

Today, I send love to these people in my life...

1 _____
2 _____
3 _____

Powerful Positive Affirmation

I CAN BE WHATEVER I WANT TO BE.

Gratitude
Today, I am so happy and grateful for...

1 _____
2 _____
3 _____
4 _____
5 _____

6 _____
7 _____
8 _____
9 _____
10 _____

Self-Image
Today, I am...

_____
_____
_____

Inspired Action
Today, I take these actions towards my goals...

1 _____
2 _____
3 _____

4 _____
5 _____
6 _____

Sending Love
Today, I send love to these people in my life...

1 _____
2 _____
3 _____

Powerful Positive Affirmation

I AM DRIVEN BY THE SPARKLING VISION OF MY FUTURE.

Gratitude
Today, I am so happy and grateful for...

1 _____
2 _____
3 _____
4 _____
5 _____

6 _____
7 _____
8 _____
9 _____
10 _____

Self-Image
Today, I am...

_____

_____

_____

Inspired Action
Today, I take these actions towards my goals...

1 _____
2 _____
3 _____

4 _____
5 _____
6 _____

Sending Love
Today, I send love to these people in my life...

1 _____
2 _____
3 _____

Powerful Positive Affirmation

I AM INSPIRED TO LEARN AND GROW.

Gratitude

Today, I am so happy and grateful for...

1 _____   6 _____

2 _____   7 _____

3 _____   8 _____

4 _____   9 _____

5 _____   10 _____

Self-Image

Today, I am...

_____

_____

_____

Inspired Action

Today, I take these actions towards my goals...

1 _____   4 _____

2 _____   5 _____

3 _____   6 _____

Sending Love

Today, I send love to these people in my life...

1 _____

2 _____

3 _____

Powerful Positive Affirmation

TODAY WILL BE A PRODUCTIVE DAY.

Gratitude
Today, I am so happy and grateful for...

1 _____   6 _____
2 _____   7 _____
3 _____   8 _____
4 _____   9 _____
5 _____   10 _____

Self-Image
Today, I am...

_____

_____

_____

Inspired Action
Today, I take these actions towards my goals...

1 _____   4 _____
2 _____   5 _____
3 _____   6 _____

Sending Love
Today, I send love to these people in my life...

1 _____
2 _____
3 _____

Powerful Positive Affirmation

I AM INTELLIGENT AND FOCUSED.

Gratitude
Today, I am so happy and grateful for...

1 _____   6 _____

2 _____   7 _____

3 _____   8 _____

4 _____   9 _____

5 _____   10 _____

Self-Image
Today, I am...

_____

_____

_____

Inspired Action
Today, I take these actions towards my goals...

1 _____   4 _____

2 _____   5 _____

3 _____   6 _____

Sending Love
Today, I send love to these people in my life...

1 _____

2 _____

3 _____

Powerful Positive Affirmation

I FEEL MORE GRATEFUL EACH DAY.

Gratitude
Today, I am so happy and grateful for...

1 _____ 6 _____
2 _____ 7 _____
3 _____ 8 _____
4 _____ 9 _____
5 _____ 10 _____

Self-Image
Today, I am...

_____
_____
_____

Inspired Action
Today, I take these actions towards my goals...

1 _____ 4 _____
2 _____ 5 _____
3 _____ 6 _____

Sending Love
Today, I send love to these people in my life...

1 _____
2 _____
3 _____

Powerful Positive Affirmation

I AM GETTING HEALTHIER EVERY DAY.

Gratitude
Today, I am so happy and grateful for...

1 _____   6 _____

2 _____   7 _____

3 _____   8 _____

4 _____   9 _____

5 _____   10 _____

Self-Image
Today, I am...

_____

_____

_____

Inspired Action
Today, I take these actions towards my goals...

1 _____   4 _____

2 _____   5 _____

3 _____   6 _____

Sending Love
Today, I send love to these people in my life...

1 _____

2 _____

3 _____

Powerful Positive Affirmation

EACH AND EVERY DAY, I AM GETTING CLOSER TO ACHIEVING MY GOALS.

Gratitude
Today, I am so happy and grateful for...

1 _____   6 _____
2 _____   7 _____
3 _____   8 _____
4 _____   9 _____
5 _____   10 _____

Self-Image
Today, I am...

_____

_____

_____

Inspired Action
Today, I take these actions towards my goals...

1 _____   4 _____
2 _____   5 _____
3 _____   6 _____

Sending Love
Today, I send love to these people in my life...

1 _____
2 _____
3 _____

Powerful Positive Affirmation

THROUGH THE POWER OF MY THOUGHTS AND WORDS, INCREDIBLE TRANSFORMATIONS ARE HAPPENING IN ME AND WITHIN MY LIFE RIGHT NOW.

Gratitude
Today, I am so happy and grateful for...

1 _____ 6 _____

2 _____ 7 _____

3 _____ 8 _____

4 _____ 9 _____

5 _____ 10 _____

Self-Image
Today, I am...

_____

_____

_____

Inspired Action
Today, I take these actions towards my goals...

1 _____ 4 _____

2 _____ 5 _____

3 _____ 6 _____

Sending Love
Today, I send love to these people in my life...

1 _____

2 _____

3 _____

Powerful Positive Affirmation

I AM CONSTANTLY GROWING AND EVOLVING.

Gratitude
Today, I am so happy and grateful for...

1 _____   6 _____
2 _____   7 _____
3 _____   8 _____
4 _____   9 _____
5 _____   10 _____

Self-Image
Today, I am...

_____
_____
_____

Inspired Action
Today, I take these actions towards my goals...

1 _____   4 _____
2 _____   5 _____
3 _____   6 _____

Sending Love
Today, I send love to these people in my life...

1 _____
2 _____
3 _____

Powerful Positive Affirmation

WITH SELF-LOVE, I FREE MYSELF.

Gratitude
Today, I am so happy and grateful for...

1 _____
2 _____
3 _____
4 _____
5 _____

6 _____
7 _____
8 _____
9 _____
10 _____

Self-Image
Today, I am...

_____

_____

_____

Inspired Action
Today, I take these actions towards my goals...

1 _____
2 _____
3 _____

4 _____
5 _____
6 _____

Sending Love
Today, I send love to these people in my life...

1 _____
2 _____
3 _____

Powerful Positive Affirmation

I ACCEPT MYSELF FOR WHO I AM
AND CREATE PEACE, POWER AND
CONFIDENCE OF MIND AND OF HEART.

Gratitude

Today, I am so happy and grateful for...

1 _____   6 _____

2 _____   7 _____

3 _____   8 _____

4 _____   9 _____

5 _____   10 _____

Self-Image

Today, I am...

_____

_____

_____

Inspired Action

Today, I take these actions towards my goals...

1 _____   4 _____

2 _____   5 _____

3 _____   6 _____

Sending Love

Today, I send love to these people in my life...

1 _____

2 _____

3 _____

Powerful Positive Affirmation

I FORGIVE EVERYTHING AND
SET MYSELF FREE BY LETTING GO.

Gratitude
Today, I am so happy and grateful for...

1 _____   6 _____
2 _____   7 _____
3 _____   8 _____
4 _____   9 _____
5 _____   10 _____

Self-Image
Today, I am...

_____
_____
_____

Inspired Action
Today, I take these actions towards my goals...

1 _____   4 _____
2 _____   5 _____
3 _____   6 _____

Sending Love
Today, I send love to these people in my life...

1 _____
2 _____
3 _____

Powerful Positive Affirmation

I AM HEALING AND STRENGTHENING EVERY DAY.

Gratitude
Today, I am so happy and grateful for...

1 _____   6 _____
2 _____   7 _____
3 _____   8 _____
4 _____   9 _____
5 _____   10 _____

Self-Image
Today, I am...

_____
_____
_____

Inspired Action
Today, I take these actions towards my goals...

1 _____   4 _____
2 _____   5 _____
3 _____   6 _____

Sending Love
Today, I send love to these people in my life...

1 _____
2 _____
3 _____

Powerful Positive Affirmation

I SQUEEZE EVERY OUNCE OF VALUE OUT OF EACH OF MY DAYS ON THIS PLANET —TODAY, TOMORROW, AND EVERYDAY.

Gratitude
Today, I am so happy and grateful for...

1 _____   6 _____

2 _____   7 _____

3 _____   8 _____

4 _____   9 _____

5 _____   10 _____

Self-Image
Today, I am...

_____

_____

_____

Inspired Action
Today, I take these actions towards my goals...

1 _____   4 _____

2 _____   5 _____

3 _____   6 _____

Sending Love
Today, I send love to these people in my life...

1 _____

2 _____

3 _____

Powerful Positive Affirmation

I AM AWARE OF THE INCREDIBLE POWER
I POSSESS WITHIN ME TO
ACHIEVE ANYTHING I DESIRE.

Gratitude
Today, I am so happy and grateful for...

1 _____
2 _____
3 _____
4 _____
5 _____

6 _____
7 _____
8 _____
9 _____
10 _____

Self-Image
Today, I am...

_____

_____

_____

Inspired Action
Today, I take these actions towards my goals...

1 _____
2 _____
3 _____

4 _____
5 _____
6 _____

Sending Love
Today, I send love to these people in my life...

1 _____
2 _____
3 _____

Powerful Positive Affirmation

I CONTINOUSLY STEP INTO MY EXPANSION.

Gratitude

Today, I am so happy and grateful for...

1 _____
2 _____
3 _____
4 _____
5 _____

6 _____
7 _____
8 _____
9 _____
10 _____

Self-Image

Today, I am...

_____

_____

_____

Inspired Action

Today, I take these actions towards my goals...

1 _____
2 _____
3 _____

4 _____
5 _____
6 _____

Sending Love

Today, I send love to these people in my life...

1 _____
2 _____
3 _____

Powerful Positive Affirmation

AS I STEP INTO EXPANSIVE FEELINGS, I NATURALLY TURN AWAY FROM CONTRACTIVE FEELINGS.

Gratitude

Today, I am so happy and grateful for...

1 _____   6 _____

2 _____   7 _____

3 _____   8 _____

4 _____   9 _____

5 _____   10 _____

Self-Image

Today, I am...

_____

_____

_____

Inspired Action

Today, I take these actions towards my goals...

1 _____   4 _____

2 _____   5 _____

3 _____   6 _____

Sending Love

Today, I send love to these people in my life...

1 _____

2 _____

3 _____

Powerful Positive Affirmation

I BELONG IN THIS WORLD;
THERE ARE PEOPLE THAT
CARE ABOUT ME AND MY WORTH.

Gratitude
Today, I am so happy and grateful for...

1 _____   6 _____
2 _____   7 _____
3 _____   8 _____
4 _____   9 _____
5 _____   10 _____

Self-Image
Today, I am...

_____

_____

_____

Inspired Action
Today, I take these actions towards my goals...

1 _____   4 _____
2 _____   5 _____
3 _____   6 _____

Sending Love
Today, I send love to these people in my life...

1 _____
2 _____
3 _____

Powerful Positive Affirmation

MY SOUL RADIATES FROM THE INSIDE
AND WARMS THE SOULS OF OTHERS.

Day   Month   Year

Gratitude
Today, I am so happy and grateful for...

1 _____   6 _____
2 _____   7 _____
3 _____   8 _____
4 _____   9 _____
5 _____   10 _____

Self-Image
Today, I am...

_____
_____
_____

Inspired Action
Today, I take these actions towards my goals...

1 _____   4 _____
2 _____   5 _____
3 _____   6 _____

Sending Love
Today, I send love to these people in my life...

1 _____
2 _____
3 _____

Powerful Positive Affirmation

NOTE TO SELF: I AM PROUD OF YOU.

Gratitude
Today, I am so happy and grateful for...

1 _____   6 _____
2 _____   7 _____
3 _____   8 _____
4 _____   9 _____
5 _____   10 _____

Self-Image
Today, I am...

_____

_____

_____

Inspired Action
Today, I take these actions towards my goals...

1 _____   4 _____
2 _____   5 _____
3 _____   6 _____

Sending Love
Today, I send love to these people in my life...

1 _____
2 _____
3 _____

Powerful Positive Affirmation

I INVEST IN WHAT MATTERS
AND LET GO OF WHAT DOES NOT.

Gratitude

Today, I am so happy and grateful for...

1 _____   6 _____
2 _____   7 _____
3 _____   8 _____
4 _____   9 _____
5 _____   10 _____

Self-Image
Today, I am...

_____
_____
_____

Inspired Action
Today, I take these actions towards my goals...

1 _____   4 _____
2 _____   5 _____
3 _____   6 _____

Sending Love
Today, I send love to these people in my life...

1 _____
2 _____
3 _____

Powerful Positive Affirmation

I FEED MY SPIRIT.
I TRAIN MY BODY.
I FOCUS MY MIND.

Gratitude
Today, I am so happy and grateful for...

1 _____ 6 _____
2 _____ 7 _____
3 _____ 8 _____
4 _____ 9 _____
5 _____ 10 _____

Self-Image
Today, I am...

_____

_____

_____

Inspired Action
Today, I take these actions towards my goals...

1 _____ 4 _____
2 _____ 5 _____
3 _____ 6 _____

Sending Love
Today, I send love to these people in my life...

1 _____
2 _____
3 _____

Powerful Positive Affirmation

THIS IS MY TIME.

Gratitude

Today, I am so happy and grateful for...

1 _____   6 _____

2 _____   7 _____

3 _____   8 _____

4 _____   9 _____

5 _____   10 _____

Self-Image

Today, I am...

_____

_____

_____

Inspired Action

Today, I take these actions towards my goals...

1 _____   4 _____

2 _____   5 _____

3 _____   6 _____

Sending Love

Today, I send love to these people in my life...

1 _____

2 _____

3 _____

Powerful Positive Affirmation

MY LIFE HAS MEANING.
WHAT I DO HAS MEANING.

Gratitude
Today, I am so happy and grateful for...

1 _____   6 _____
2 _____   7 _____
3 _____   8 _____
4 _____   9 _____
5 _____   10 _____

Self-Image
Today, I am...

_____

_____

_____

Inspired Action
Today, I take these actions towards my goals...

1 _____   4 _____
2 _____   5 _____
3 _____   6 _____

Sending Love
Today, I send love to these people in my life...

1 _____
2 _____
3 _____

Powerful Positive Affirmation

I AM MADE OF LOVE.

Gratitude

Today, I am so happy and grateful for...

1 _____   6 _____
2 _____   7 _____
3 _____   8 _____
4 _____   9 _____
5 _____   10 _____

Self-Image
Today, I am...

_____

_____

_____

Inspired Action
Today, I take these actions towards my goals...

1 _____   4 _____
2 _____   5 _____
3 _____   6 _____

Sending Love
Today, I send love to these people in my life...

1 _____

2 _____

3 _____

Powerful Positive Affirmation

WHAT I THINK ABOUT I BRING ABOUT.

Gratitude

Today, I am so happy and grateful for...

1 _____   6 _____
2 _____   7 _____
3 _____   8 _____
4 _____   9 _____
5 _____   10 _____

Self-Image
Today, I am...

_____

_____

_____

Inspired Action
Today, I take these actions towards my goals...

1 _____   4 _____
2 _____   5 _____
3 _____   6 _____

Sending Love
Today, I send love to these people in my life...

1 _____
2 _____
3 _____

Powerful Positive Affirmation

I AM THE PERFECT EXPRESSION OF HEALTH.

Gratitude

Today, I am so happy and grateful for...

1 _____   6 _____
2 _____   7 _____
3 _____   8 _____
4 _____   9 _____
5 _____   10 _____

Self-Image

Today, I am...

_____

_____

_____

Inspired Action

Today, I take these actions towards my goals...

1 _____   4 _____
2 _____   5 _____
3 _____   6 _____

Sending Love

Today, I send love to these people in my life...

1 _____
2 _____
3 _____

Powerful Positive Affirmation

I AM GRATEFUL FOR AN ABUNDANCE OF FOCUSED ENERGY THAT ALLOWS ME TO COMPLETE EACH AND EVERY TASK EFFORTLESSLY WITH JOY AND CONFIDENCE.

Gratitude
Today, I am so happy and grateful for...

1 _____   6 _____
2 _____   7 _____
3 _____   8 _____
4 _____   9 _____
5 _____   10 _____

Self-Image
Today, I am...

_____

_____

_____

Inspired Action
Today, I take these actions towards my goals...

1 _____   4 _____
2 _____   5 _____
3 _____   6 _____

Sending Love
Today, I send love to these people in my life...

1 _____
2 _____
3 _____

Powerful Positive Affirmation

I ASSIMILATE NEW IDEAS EASILY AND EFFORTLESSLY, AND EXPRESS THEM CREATIVELY AND INTELLIGENTLY.

Gratitude

Today, I am so happy and grateful for...

1 _____   6 _____

2 _____   7 _____

3 _____   8 _____

4 _____   9 _____

5 _____   10 _____

Self-Image

Today, I am...

_____

_____

_____

Inspired Action

Today, I take these actions towards my goals...

1 _____   4 _____

2 _____   5 _____

3 _____   6 _____

Sending Love

Today, I send love to these people in my life...

1 _____

2 _____

3 _____

Powerful Positive Affirmation

MY BODY IS FUNCTIONING HARMONIOUSLY.

Gratitude
Today, I am so happy and grateful for...

1 _____   6 _____
2 _____   7 _____
3 _____   8 _____
4 _____   9 _____
5 _____   10 _____

Self-Image
Today, I am...

_____
_____
_____

Inspired Action
Today, I take these actions towards my goals...

1 _____   4 _____
2 _____   5 _____
3 _____   6 _____

Sending Love
Today, I send love to these people in my life...

1 _____
2 _____
3 _____

Powerful Positive Affirmation

MY BODY, MIND AND SPIRIT
ARE IN PERFECT ALIGNMENT.

Gratitude
Today, I am so happy and grateful for...

1 _____   6 _____
2 _____   7 _____
3 _____   8 _____
4 _____   9 _____
5 _____   10 _____

Self-Image
Today, I am...

_____
_____
_____

Inspired Action
Today, I take these actions towards my goals...

1 _____   4 _____
2 _____   5 _____
3 _____   6 _____

Sending Love
Today, I send love to these people in my life...

1 _____
2 _____
3 _____

Powerful Positive Affirmation

I CAN ACHIEVE GREATNESS.

Gratitude
Today, I am so happy and grateful for...

1 _____   6 _____
2 _____   7 _____
3 _____   8 _____
4 _____   9 _____
5 _____   10 _____

Self-Image
Today, I am...

_____

_____

_____

Inspired Action
Today, I take these actions towards my goals...

1 _____   4 _____
2 _____   5 _____
3 _____   6 _____

Sending Love
Today, I send love to these people in my life...

1 _____

2 _____

3 _____

Powerful Positive Affirmation

I AM HEALTHY, ENERGETIC AND OPTIMISTIC.

Day   Month   Year

Gratitude
Today, I am so happy and grateful for...

1 _____   6 _____
2 _____   7 _____
3 _____   8 _____
4 _____   9 _____
5 _____   10 _____

Self-Image
Today, I am...

_____
_____
_____

Inspired Action
Today, I take these actions towards my goals...

1 _____   4 _____
2 _____   5 _____
3 _____   6 _____

Sending Love
Today, I send love to these people in my life...

1 _____
2 _____
3 _____

Powerful Positive Affirmation

I CHOOSE LOVE.

Gratitude

Today, I am so happy and grateful for...

1 _____   6 _____
2 _____   7 _____
3 _____   8 _____
4 _____   9 _____
5 _____   10 _____

Self-Image

Today, I am...

_____
_____
_____

Inspired Action

Today, I take these actions towards my goals...

1 _____   4 _____
2 _____   5 _____
3 _____   6 _____

Sending Love

Today, I send love to these people in my life...

1 _____
2 _____
3 _____

Powerful Positive Affirmation

HAPPINESS IS A CHOICE,
AND TODAY I CHOOSE TO BE HAPPY.

Gratitude

Today, I am so happy and grateful for...

1 _____
2 _____
3 _____
4 _____
5 _____

6 _____
7 _____
8 _____
9 _____
10 _____

Self-Image

Today, I am...

_____

_____

_____

Inspired Action

Today, I take these actions towards my goals...

1 _____
2 _____
3 _____

4 _____
5 _____
6 _____

Sending Love

Today, I send love to these people in my life...

1 _____
2 _____
3 _____

Powerful Positive Affirmation

MY SKILLS AND TALENTS TAKE ME TO PLACES THAT AMAZE ME.

Gratitude
Today, I am so happy and grateful for...

1 _____ 6 _____

2 _____ 7 _____

3 _____ 8 _____

4 _____ 9 _____

5 _____ 10 _____

Self-Image
Today, I am...

_____

_____

_____

Inspired Action
Today, I take these actions towards my goals...

1 _____ 4 _____

2 _____ 5 _____

3 _____ 6 _____

Sending Love
Today, I send love to these people in my life...

1 _____

2 _____

3 _____

Powerful Positive Affirmation

I SET GOALS AND GO AFTER THEM WITH DETERMINATION.

Gratitude
Today, I am so happy and grateful for...

1 _____   6 _____
2 _____   7 _____
3 _____   8 _____
4 _____   9 _____
5 _____   10 _____

Self-Image
Today, I am...

_____

_____

_____

Inspired Action
Today, I take these actions towards my goals...

1 _____   4 _____
2 _____   5 _____
3 _____   6 _____

Sending Love
Today, I send love to these people in my life...

1 _____
2 _____
3 _____

Powerful Positive Affirmation

I WAKE UP WITH A POWERFUL THOUGHT TO SET THE TONE AND ALLOW SUCCESS TO REVERBERATE THROUGH EVERY MOMENT OF MY DAY.

Gratitude
Today, I am so happy and grateful for...

1 _____   6 _____
2 _____   7 _____
3 _____   8 _____
4 _____   9 _____
5 _____   10 _____

Self-Image
Today, I am...

_____

_____

_____

Inspired Action
Today, I take these actions towards my goals...

1 _____   4 _____
2 _____   5 _____
3 _____   6 _____

Sending Love
Today, I send love to these people in my life...

1 _____
2 _____
3 _____

Powerful Positive Affirmation

ONE POSITIVE THOUGHT IN THE MORNING CAN CHANGE MY WHOLE DAY.

Gratitude
Today, I am so happy and grateful for...

1 _____
2 _____
3 _____
4 _____
5 _____

6 _____
7 _____
8 _____
9 _____
10 _____

Self-Image
Today, I am...

_____
_____
_____

Inspired Action
Today, I take these actions towards my goals...

1 _____
2 _____
3 _____

4 _____
5 _____
6 _____

Sending Love
Today, I send love to these people in my life...

1 _____
2 _____
3 _____

Powerful Positive Affirmation

MY ACTIONS ARE MEANINGFUL AND INSPIRING.

Gratitude
Today, I am so happy and grateful for...

1 _____   6 _____
2 _____   7 _____
3 _____   8 _____
4 _____   9 _____
5 _____   10 _____

Self-Image
Today, I am...

_____
_____
_____

Inspired Action
Today, I take these actions towards my goals...

1 _____   4 _____
2 _____   5 _____
3 _____   6 _____

Sending Love
Today, I send love to these people in my life...

1 _____
2 _____
3 _____

Powerful Positive Affirmation

EVERYTHING HAPPENS FOR A REASON. EVERYTHING LEADS TO SOMETHING POSITIVE.

Gratitude

Today, I am so happy and grateful for...

1 _____   6 _____
2 _____   7 _____
3 _____   8 _____
4 _____   9 _____
5 _____   10 _____

Self-Image

Today, I am...

_____

_____

_____

Inspired Action

Today, I take these actions towards my goals...

1 _____   4 _____
2 _____   5 _____
3 _____   6 _____

Sending Love

Today, I send love to these people in my life...

1 _____
2 _____
3 _____

Powerful Positive Affirmation

I AM FORGIVING.

Gratitude
Today, I am so happy and grateful for...

1 _____   6 _____
2 _____   7 _____
3 _____   8 _____
4 _____   9 _____
5 _____   10 _____

Self-Image
Today, I am...

_____

_____

_____

Inspired Action
Today, I take these actions towards my goals...

1 _____   4 _____
2 _____   5 _____
3 _____   6 _____

Sending Love
Today, I send love to these people in my life...

1 _____
2 _____
3 _____

Powerful Positive Affirmation

I LET GO OF ALL THOUGHTS, FEELINGS AND BELIEF THAT NO LONGER SERVE ME.

Gratitude
Today, I am so happy and grateful for...

Day   Month   Year

1 _____   6 _____
2 _____   7 _____
3 _____   8 _____
4 _____   9 _____
5 _____   10 _____

Self-Image
Today, I am...

_____
_____
_____

Inspired Action
Today, I take these actions towards my goals...

1 _____   4 _____
2 _____   5 _____
3 _____   6 _____

Sending Love
Today, I send love to these people in my life...

1 _____
2 _____
3 _____

Powerful Positive Affirmation

I MOVE BEYOND FORGIVENESS TO UNDERSTANDING, AND I HAVE COMPASSION FOR ALL.

Gratitude
Today, I am so happy and grateful for...

1 _____   6 _____
2 _____   7 _____
3 _____   8 _____
4 _____   9 _____
5 _____   10 _____

Self-Image
Today, I am...

_____
_____
_____

Inspired Action
Today, I take these actions towards my goals...

1 _____   4 _____
2 _____   5 _____
3 _____   6 _____

Sending Love
Today, I send love to these people in my life...

1 _____
2 _____
3 _____

Powerful Positive Affirmation

I AM BECOMING MORE CONFIDENT AND STRONGER EACH DAY.

Gratitude

Today, I am so happy and grateful for...

1 _____   6 _____

2 _____   7 _____

3 _____   8 _____

4 _____   9 _____

5 _____   10 _____

Self-Image
Today, I am...

_____

_____

_____

Inspired Action
Today, I take these actions towards my goals...

1 _____   4 _____

2 _____   5 _____

3 _____   6 _____

Sending Love
Today, I send love to these people in my life...

1 _____

2 _____

3 _____

Powerful Positive Affirmation

MY POTENTIAL TO SUCCEED IS INFINITE.

Gratitude
Today, I am so happy and grateful for...

1 _____ 6 _____

2 _____ 7 _____

3 _____ 8 _____

4 _____ 9 _____

5 _____ 10 _____

Self-Image
Today, I am...

_____

_____

_____

Inspired Action
Today, I take these actions towards my goals...

1 _____ 4 _____

2 _____ 5 _____

3 _____ 6 _____

Sending Love
Today, I send love to these people in my life...

1 _____

2 _____

3 _____

Powerful Positive Affirmation

I AM BECOMING MORE KNOWLEDGEABLE AND WISER WITH EACH DAY.

Gratitude

Today, I am so happy and grateful for...

1 _____   6 _____
2 _____   7 _____
3 _____   8 _____
4 _____   9 _____
5 _____   10 _____

Self-Image
Today, I am...

_____

_____

_____

Inspired Action
Today, I take these actions towards my goals...

1 _____   4 _____
2 _____   5 _____
3 _____   6 _____

Sending Love
Today, I send love to these people in my life...

1 _____
2 _____
3 _____

Powerful Positive Affirmation

I AM CREATIVE AND BURSTING WITH BRILLIANT IDEAS.

Gratitude

Today, I am so happy and grateful for...

1 _____   6 _____

2 _____   7 _____

3 _____   8 _____

4 _____   9 _____

5 _____   10 _____

Self-Image
Today, I am...

_____

_____

_____

Inspired Action
Today, I take these actions towards my goals...

1 _____   4 _____

2 _____   5 _____

3 _____   6 _____

Sending Love
Today, I send love to these people in my life...

1 _____

2 _____

3 _____

Powerful Positive Affirmation

I AM COURAGEOUS AND OVERCOME MY FEARS BY TRANSFORMING THEM INTO STEPPING STONES.

Gratitude

Today, I am so happy and grateful for...

1 _____   6 _____
2 _____   7 _____
3 _____   8 _____
4 _____   9 _____
5 _____   10 _____

Self-Image

Today, I am...

_____
_____
_____
_____

Inspired Action

Today, I take these actions towards my goals...

1 _____   4 _____
2 _____   5 _____
3 _____   6 _____

Sending Love

Today, I send love to these people in my life...

1 _____
2 _____
3 _____

Powerful Positive Affirmation

I AM AT PEACE WITH MYSELF
AND EVERYONE AROUND ME.

Gratitude

Today, I am so happy and grateful for...

1 _____   6 _____
2 _____   7 _____
3 _____   8 _____
4 _____   9 _____
5 _____   10 _____

Self-Image

Today, I am...

_____

_____

_____

Inspired Action

Today, I take these actions towards my goals...

1 _____   4 _____
2 _____   5 _____
3 _____   6 _____

Sending Love

Today, I send love to these people in my life...

1 _____
2 _____
3 _____

Powerful Positive Affirmation

I RADIATE LOVE, HAPPINESS, GRACE AND POSITIVITY.

Gratitude

Today, I am so happy and grateful for...

1 _____   6 _____

2 _____   7 _____

3 _____   8 _____

4 _____   9 _____

5 _____   10 _____

Self-Image

Today, I am...

_____

_____

_____

Inspired Action

Today, I take these actions towards my goals...

1 _____   4 _____

2 _____   5 _____

3 _____   6 _____

Sending Love

Today, I send love to these people in my life...

1 _____

2 _____

3 _____

Powerful Positive Affirmation

I AM GRATEFUL FOR THE WONDERS IN MY LIFE.

Gratitude

Today, I am so happy and grateful for...

1 _____   6 _____

2 _____   7 _____

3 _____   8 _____

4 _____   9 _____

5 _____   10 _____

Self-Image

Today, I am...

_____

_____

_____

Inspired Action

Today, I take these actions towards my goals...

1 _____   4 _____

2 _____   5 _____

3 _____   6 _____

Sending Love

Today, I send love to these people in my life...

1 _____

2 _____

3 _____

Powerful Positive Affirmation

I LOVE MYSELF THE WAY THAT I WANT OTHERS TO.

Gratitude
Today, I am so happy and grateful for...

1 _____   6 _____
2 _____   7 _____
3 _____   8 _____
4 _____   9 _____
5 _____   10 _____

Self-Image
Today, I am...

_____

_____

_____

Inspired Action
Today, I take these actions towards my goals...

1 _____   4 _____
2 _____   5 _____
3 _____   6 _____

Sending Love
Today, I send love to these people in my life...

1 _____
2 _____
3 _____

Powerful Positive Affirmation

THE UNIVERSE SUPPORTS ME
IN EVERY POSSIBLE WAY.

Gratitude
Today, I am so happy and grateful for...

1 _____   6 _____

2 _____   7 _____

3 _____   8 _____

4 _____   9 _____

5 _____ 10 _____

Self-Image
Today, I am...

_____

_____

_____

Inspired Action
Today, I take these actions towards my goals...

1 _____   4 _____

2 _____   5 _____

3 _____   6 _____

Sending Love
Today, I send love to these people in my life...

1 _____

2 _____

3 _____

Powerful Positive Affirmation

EVERY EXPERIENCE IN MY LIFE HELPS ME TO GROW.

Day   Month   Year

Gratitude
Today, I am so happy and grateful for...

1 _____   6 _____
2 _____   7 _____
3 _____   8 _____
4 _____   9 _____
5 _____   10 _____

Self-Image
Today, I am...

_____
_____
_____

Inspired Action
Today, I take these actions towards my goals...

1 _____   4 _____
2 _____   5 _____
3 _____   6 _____

Sending Love
Today, I send love to these people in my life...

1 _____
2 _____
3 _____

Powerful Positive Affirmation

TODAY, I LAY THE FOUNDATION
FOR A WONDERFUL FUTURE.

Gratitude
Today, I am so happy and grateful for...

1 _____   6 _____

2 _____   7 _____

3 _____   8 _____

4 _____   9 _____

5 _____   10 _____

Self-Image
Today, I am...

_____

_____

_____

Inspired Action
Today, I take these actions towards my goals...

1 _____   4 _____

2 _____   5 _____

3 _____   6 _____

Sending Love
Today, I send love to these people in my life...

1 _____

2 _____

3 _____

Powerful Positive Affirmation

I SPEAK KINDLY OF OTHERS.

Gratitude

Today, I am so happy and grateful for...

1 _____   6 _____
2 _____   7 _____
3 _____   8 _____
4 _____   9 _____
5 _____   10 _____

Self-Image

Today, I am...

_____
_____
_____

Inspired Action

Today, I take these actions towards my goals...

1 _____   4 _____
2 _____   5 _____
3 _____   6 _____

Sending Love

Today, I send love to these people in my life...

1 _____
2 _____
3 _____

Powerful Positive Affirmation

ONLY I HAVE CONTROL OVER MYSELF AND MY CHOICES.

Gratitude

Today, I am so happy and grateful for...

1 _____   6 _____

2 _____   7 _____

3 _____   8 _____

4 _____   9 _____

5 _____   10 _____

Self-Image

Today, I am...

_____

_____

_____

Inspired Action

Today, I take these actions towards my goals...

1 _____   4 _____

2 _____   5 _____

3 _____   6 _____

Sending Love

Today, I send love to these people in my life...

1 _____

2 _____

3 _____

Powerful Positive Affirmation

EVERYTHING I SEEK CAN BE FOUND WITHIN.

Gratitude

Today, I am so happy and grateful for...

1 _____   6 _____

2 _____   7 _____

3 _____   8 _____

4 _____   9 _____

5 _____   10 _____

Self-Image

Today, I am...

_____

_____

_____

Inspired Action

Today, I take these actions towards my goals...

1 _____   4 _____

2 _____   5 _____

3 _____   6 _____

Sending Love

Today, I send love to these people in my life...

1 _____

2 _____

3 _____

Powerful Positive Affirmation

I SET MYSELF FREE BY FORGIVING MYSELF.

Gratitude

Today, I am so happy and grateful for...

1 _____   6 _____

2 _____   7 _____

3 _____   8 _____

4 _____   9 _____

5 _____   10 _____

Self-Image

Today, I am...

_____

_____

_____

Inspired Action

Today, I take these actions towards my goals...

1 _____   4 _____

2 _____   5 _____

3 _____   6 _____

Sending Love

Today, I send love to these people in my life...

1 _____

2 _____

3 _____

Powerful Positive Affirmation

I AM SPECIAL, UNIQUE AND
THE ONLY 'ME' IN THE UNIVERSE.

Gratitude
Today, I am so happy and grateful for...

1 _____
2 _____
3 _____
4 _____
5 _____

6 _____
7 _____
8 _____
9 _____
10 _____

Self-Image
Today, I am...

_____

_____

_____

Inspired Action
Today, I take these actions towards my goals...

1 _____
2 _____
3 _____

4 _____
5 _____
6 _____

Sending Love
Today, I send love to these people in my life...

1 _____
2 _____
3 _____

Powerful Positive Affirmation

I CREATE A LIFE THAT MAKES ME EXCITED TO GET OUT OF BED EACH DAY.

Gratitude
Today, I am so happy and grateful for...

1 _____ 6 _____

2 _____ 7 _____

3 _____ 8 _____

4 _____ 9 _____

5 _____ 10 _____

Self-Image
Today, I am...

_____

_____

_____

Inspired Action
Today, I take these actions towards my goals...

1 _____ 4 _____

2 _____ 5 _____

3 _____ 6 _____

Sending Love
Today, I send love to these people in my life...

1 _____

2 _____

3 _____

Powerful Positive Affirmation

I GIVE MYSELF PERMISSION TO GO AFTER WHAT I WANT.

Gratitude
Today, I am so happy and grateful for...

1 _____   6 _____
2 _____   7 _____
3 _____   8 _____
4 _____   9 _____
5 _____   10 _____

Self-Image
Today, I am...

_____

_____

_____

Inspired Action
Today, I take these actions towards my goals...

1 _____   4 _____
2 _____   5 _____
3 _____   6 _____

Sending Love
Today, I send love to these people in my life...

1 _____
2 _____
3 _____

Powerful Positive Affirmation

I LOVE MYSELF AND FEEL GREAT ABOUT MYSELF.

Gratitude
Today, I am so happy and grateful for...

1 _____   6 _____
2 _____   7 _____
3 _____   8 _____
4 _____   9 _____
5 _____   10 _____

Self-Image
Today, I am...

_____

_____

_____

Inspired Action
Today, I take these actions towards my goals...

1 _____   4 _____
2 _____   5 _____
3 _____   6 _____

Sending Love
Today, I send love to these people in my life...

1 _____
2 _____
3 _____

Powerful Positive Affirmation

I ACCEPT AND LOVE MYSELF UNCONDITIONALLY.

Gratitude

Today, I am so happy and grateful for...

1 _____   6 _____

2 _____   7 _____

3 _____   8 _____

4 _____   9 _____

5 _____   10 _____

Self-Image

Today, I am...

_____

_____

_____

Inspired Action

Today, I take these actions towards my goals...

1 _____   4 _____

2 _____   5 _____

3 _____   6 _____

Sending Love

Today, I send love to these people in my life...

1 _____

2 _____

3 _____

Powerful Positive Affirmation

I SEE PROBLEMS AS INTERESTING CHALLENGES AND OPPORTUNITIES FOR GROWTH.

Gratitude

Today, I am so happy and grateful for...

1 _____
2 _____
3 _____
4 _____
5 _____

6 _____
7 _____
8 _____
9 _____
10 _____

Self-Image

Today, I am...

_____

_____

_____

Inspired Action

Today, I take these actions towards my goals...

1 _____
2 _____
3 _____

4 _____
5 _____
6 _____

Sending Love

Today, I send love to these people in my life...

1 _____
2 _____
3 _____

Powerful Positive Affirmation

I RADIATE CONFIDENCE.

Gratitude
Today, I am so happy and grateful for...

1 _____   6 _____
2 _____   7 _____
3 _____   8 _____
4 _____   9 _____
5 _____   10 _____

Self-Image
Today, I am...

_____

_____

_____

Inspired Action
Today, I take these actions towards my goals...

1 _____   4 _____
2 _____   5 _____
3 _____   6 _____

Sending Love
Today, I send love to these people in my life...

1 _____

2 _____

3 _____

Powerful Positive Affirmation

CHALLENGES BRING OUT THE BEST IN ME.

Gratitude

Today, I am so happy and grateful for...

1 _____ 6 _____
2 _____ 7 _____
3 _____ 8 _____
4 _____ 9 _____
5 _____ 10 _____

Self-Image

Today, I am...

_____
_____
_____

Inspired Action

Today, I take these actions towards my goals...

1 _____ 4 _____
2 _____ 5 _____
3 _____ 6 _____

Sending Love

Today, I send love to these people in my life...

1 _____
2 _____
3 _____

Powerful Positive Affirmation

I HAVE CONFIDENCE IN MY ABILITIES AND SKILLS.

Gratitude
Today, I am so happy and grateful for...

1 _____   6 _____
2 _____   7 _____
3 _____   8 _____
4 _____   9 _____
5 _____   10 _____

Self-Image
Today, I am...

_____

_____

_____

Inspired Action
Today, I take these actions towards my goals...

1 _____   4 _____
2 _____   5 _____
3 _____   6 _____

Sending Love
Today, I send love to these people in my life...

1 _____
2 _____
3 _____

Powerful Positive Affirmation

I MAKE SOUND DECISIONS THAT ARE IN MY BEST SELF-INTEREST.

Gratitude
Today, I am so happy and grateful for...

1 _____   6 _____
2 _____   7 _____
3 _____   8 _____
4 _____   9 _____
5 _____   10 _____

Self-Image
Today, I am...

_____
_____
_____

Inspired Action
Today, I take these actions towards my goals...

1 _____   4 _____
2 _____   5 _____
3 _____   6 _____

Sending Love
Today, I send love to these people in my life...

1 _____
2 _____
3 _____

Powerful Positive Affirmation

I AM BOLD AND COURAGEOUS.

Gratitude

Today, I am so happy and grateful for...

1 _____   6 _____

2 _____   7 _____

3 _____   8 _____

4 _____   9 _____

5 _____   10 _____

Self-Image

Today, I am...

_____

_____

_____

Inspired Action

Today, I take these actions towards my goals...

1 _____   4 _____

2 _____   5 _____

3 _____   6 _____

Sending Love

Today, I send love to these people in my life...

1 _____

2 _____

3 _____

Powerful Positive Affirmation

I AM WORTHY OF HAPPINESS AND LOVE.

Gratitude
Today, I am so happy and grateful for...

1 _____   6 _____

2 _____   7 _____

3 _____   8 _____

4 _____   9 _____

5 _____   10 _____

Self-Image
Today, I am...

_____

_____

_____

Inspired Action
Today, I take these actions towards my goals...

1 _____   4 _____

2 _____   5 _____

3 _____   6 _____

Sending Love
Today, I send love to these people in my life...

1 _____

2 _____

3 _____

Powerful Positive Affirmation

MY HEART IS OPEN.

Gratitude
Today, I am so happy and grateful for...

1 _____   6 _____

2 _____   7 _____

3 _____   8 _____

4 _____   9 _____

5 _____   10 _____

Self-Image
Today, I am...

_____

_____

_____

Inspired Action
Today, I take these actions towards my goals...

1 _____   4 _____

2 _____   5 _____

3 _____   6 _____

Sending Love
Today, I send love to these people in my life...

1 _____

2 _____

3 _____

Powerful Positive Affirmation

MY MIND AND MY HEART WILL REMAIN OPEN TODAY.

Gratitude
Today, I am so happy and grateful for...

1 _____   6 _____
2 _____   7 _____
3 _____   8 _____
4 _____   9 _____
5 _____   10 _____

Self-Image
Today, I am...

_____

_____

_____

Inspired Action
Today, I take these actions towards my goals...

1 _____   4 _____
2 _____   5 _____
3 _____   6 _____

Sending Love
Today, I send love to these people in my life...

1 _____
2 _____
3 _____

Powerful Positive Affirmation

I AM KIND TO EVERY PERSON I MEET.

Gratitude
Today, I am so happy and grateful for...

1 _____
2 _____
3 _____
4 _____
5 _____

6 _____
7 _____
8 _____
9 _____
10 _____

Self-Image
Today, I am...

_____

_____

_____

Inspired Action
Today, I take these actions towards my goals...

1 _____
2 _____
3 _____

4 _____
5 _____
6 _____

Sending Love
Today, I send love to these people in my life...

1 _____

2 _____

3 _____

Powerful Positive Affirmation

I AM SURROUNDED BY LOVE.

Gratitude
Today, I am so happy and grateful for...

1 _____
2 _____
3 _____
4 _____
5 _____

6 _____
7 _____
8 _____
9 _____
10 _____

Self-Image
Today, I am...

_____
_____
_____

Inspired Action
Today, I take these actions towards my goals...

1 _____
2 _____
3 _____

4 _____
5 _____
6 _____

Sending Love
Today, I send love to these people in my life...

1 _____
2 _____
3 _____

Powerful Positive Affirmation

I ATTRACT KIND PEOPLE.

Gratitude

Today, I am so happy and grateful for...

1 _____   6 _____

2 _____   7 _____

3 _____   8 _____

4 _____   9 _____

5 _____   10 _____

Self-Image

Today, I am...

_____

_____

_____

Inspired Action

Today, I take these actions towards my goals...

1 _____   4 _____

2 _____   5 _____

3 _____   6 _____

Sending Love

Today, I send love to these people in my life...

1 _____

2 _____

3 _____

Powerful Positive Affirmation

I LOVE MYSELF UNCONDITIONALLY.

Gratitude
Today, I am so happy and grateful for...

1 _____   6 _____
2 _____   7 _____
3 _____   8 _____
4 _____   9 _____
5 _____   10 _____

Self-Image
Today, I am...

_____
_____
_____

Inspired Action
Today, I take these actions towards my goals...

1 _____   4 _____
2 _____   5 _____
3 _____   6 _____

Sending Love
Today, I send love to these people in my life...

1 _____
2 _____
3 _____

Powerful Positive Affirmation

I DESERVE LOVE.

Gratitude

Today, I am so happy and grateful for...

1 _____   6 _____

2 _____   7 _____

3 _____   8 _____

4 _____   9 _____

5 _____   10 _____

Self-Image

Today, I am...

_____

_____

_____

Inspired Action

Today, I take these actions towards my goals...

1 _____   4 _____

2 _____   5 _____

3 _____   6 _____

Sending Love

Today, I send love to these people in my life...

1 _____

2 _____

3 _____

Powerful Positive Affirmation

I AM LOVED AND APPRECIATED BY THOSE AROUND ME.

Gratitude

Today, I am so happy and grateful for...

1 _____
2 _____
3 _____
4 _____
5 _____

6 _____
7 _____
8 _____
9 _____
10 _____

Self-Image

Today, I am...

_____

_____

_____

Inspired Action

Today, I take these actions towards my goals...

1 _____
2 _____
3 _____

4 _____
5 _____
6 _____

Sending Love

Today, I send love to these people in my life...

1 _____
2 _____
3 _____

Powerful Positive Affirmation

EVERYWHERE I GO, I AM ACCOMPANIED BY LOVE.

Gratitude

Today, I am so happy and grateful for...

1 _____   6 _____

2 _____   7 _____

3 _____   8 _____

4 _____   9 _____

5 _____   10 _____

Self-Image

Today, I am...

_____

_____

_____

Inspired Action

Today, I take these actions towards my goals...

1 _____   4 _____

2 _____   5 _____

3 _____   6 _____

Sending Love

Today, I send love to these people in my life...

1 _____

2 _____

3 _____

Powerful Positive Affirmation

LOVE, FORGIVENESS AND UNDERSTANDING IS THE VERY FOUNDATION OF MY RELATIONSHIP.

Gratitude
Today, I am so happy and grateful for...

1 _____   6 _____

2 _____   7 _____

3 _____   8 _____

4 _____   9 _____

5 _____   10 _____

Self-Image
Today, I am...

_____

_____

_____

Inspired Action
Today, I take these actions towards my goals...

1 _____   4 _____

2 _____   5 _____

3 _____   6 _____

Sending Love
Today, I send love to these people in my life...

1 _____

2 _____

3 _____

Powerful Positive Affirmation

I GIVE AND RECEIVE LOVE EQUALLY.

Gratitude

Today, I am so happy and grateful for...

1 _____   6 _____

2 _____   7 _____

3 _____   8 _____

4 _____   9 _____

5 _____   10 _____

Self-Image

Today, I am...

_____

_____

_____

Inspired Action

Today, I take these actions towards my goals...

1 _____   4 _____

2 _____   5 _____

3 _____   6 _____

Sending Love

Today, I send love to these people in my life...

1 _____

2 _____

3 _____

Powerful Positive Affirmation

I KNOW MYSELF, AND I AM TRUE TO MYSELF.

Gratitude
Today, I am so happy and grateful for...

1 _____
2 _____
3 _____
4 _____
5 _____

6 _____
7 _____
8 _____
9 _____
10 _____

Self-Image
Today, I am...

_____

_____

_____

Inspired Action
Today, I take these actions towards my goals...

1 _____
2 _____
3 _____

4 _____
5 _____
6 _____

Sending Love
Today, I send love to these people in my life...

1 _____
2 _____
3 _____

Powerful Positive Affirmation

I AM TREASURED FOR WHO I REALLY AM.

Gratitude

Today, I am so happy and grateful for...

1 _____ 6 _____

2 _____ 7 _____

3 _____ 8 _____

4 _____ 9 _____

5 _____ 10 _____

Self-Image
Today, I am...

_____

_____

_____

Inspired Action
Today, I take these actions towards my goals...

1 _____ 4 _____

2 _____ 5 _____

3 _____ 6 _____

Sending Love
Today, I send love to these people in my life...

1 _____

2 _____

3 _____

Powerful Positive Affirmation

MY RELATIONSHIPS ARE BECOMING STRONGER, DEEPER AND MORE LOVING WITH EVERY DAY.

Gratitude
Today, I am so happy and grateful for...

1 _____   6 _____
2 _____   7 _____
3 _____   8 _____
4 _____   9 _____
5 _____   10 _____

Self-Image
Today, I am...

_____

_____

_____

Inspired Action
Today, I take these actions towards my goals...

1 _____   4 _____
2 _____   5 _____
3 _____   6 _____

Sending Love
Today, I send love to these people in my life...

1 _____
2 _____
3 _____

Powerful Positive Affirmation

I ATTRACT MONEY EFFORTLESSLY AND EASILY.

Day   Month   Year

Gratitude
Today, I am so happy and grateful for...

1 _____   6 _____
2 _____   7 _____
3 _____   8 _____
4 _____   9 _____
5 _____   10 _____

Self-Image
Today, I am...

_____
_____
_____

Inspired Action
Today, I take these actions towards my goals...

1 _____   4 _____
2 _____   5 _____
3 _____   6 _____

Sending Love
Today, I send love to these people in my life...

1 _____
2 _____
3 _____

Powerful Positive Affirmation

I CONTINUOUSLY DISCOVER
NEW AVENUES OF INCOME.

Gratitude
Today, I am so happy and grateful for...

1 _____   6 _____
2 _____   7 _____
3 _____   8 _____
4 _____   9 _____
5 _____   10 _____

Self-Image
Today, I am...

_____
_____
_____

Inspired Action
Today, I take these actions towards my goals...

1 _____   4 _____
2 _____   5 _____
3 _____   6 _____

Sending Love
Today, I send love to these people in my life...

1 _____
2 _____
3 _____

Powerful Positive Affirmation

I AM OPEN TO ALL THE WEALTH LIFE HAS TO OFFER.

Gratitude
Today, I am so happy and grateful for...

1 _____ 6 _____
2 _____ 7 _____
3 _____ 8 _____
4 _____ 9 _____
5 _____ 10 _____

Self-Image
Today, I am...

_____
_____
_____

Inspired Action
Today, I take these actions towards my goals...

1 _____ 4 _____
2 _____ 5 _____
3 _____ 6 _____

Sending Love
Today, I send love to these people in my life...

1 _____
2 _____
3 _____

Powerful Positive Affirmation

I ATTRACT LUCRATIVE OPPORTUNITIES TO CREATE MONEY.

Gratitude
Today, I am so happy and grateful for...

1 _____   6 _____
2 _____   7 _____
3 _____   8 _____
4 _____   9 _____
5 _____   10 _____

Self-Image
Today, I am...

_____

_____

_____

Inspired Action
Today, I take these actions towards my goals...

1 _____   4 _____
2 _____   5 _____
3 _____   6 _____

Sending Love
Today, I send love to these people in my life...

1 _____

2 _____

3 _____

Powerful Positive Affirmation

I SEE ABUNDANCE EVERYWHERE.

Gratitude
Today, I am so happy and grateful for...

1 _____   6 _____
2 _____   7 _____
3 _____   8 _____
4 _____   9 _____
5 _____   10 _____

Self-Image
Today, I am...

_____
_____
_____

Inspired Action
Today, I take these actions towards my goals...

1 _____   4 _____
2 _____   5 _____
3 _____   6 _____

Sending Love
Today, I send love to these people in my life...

1 _____
2 _____
3 _____

Powerful Positive Affirmation

I AM BECOMING MORE AND MORE PROSPEROUS WITH EVERY DAY.

Gratitude

Today, I am so happy and grateful for...

1 _____   6 _____

2 _____   7. _____

3 _____   8 _____

4 _____   9 _____

5 _____   10 _____

Self-Image

Today, I am...

_____

_____

_____

Inspired Action

Today, I take these actions towards my goals...

1 _____   4 _____

2 _____   5 _____

3 _____   6 _____

Sending Love

Today, I send love to these people in my life...

1 _____

2 _____

3 _____

Powerful Positive Affirmation

MY LIFE IS FULL OF PROSPERITY.

Gratitude
Today, I am so happy and grateful for...

1 _____   6 _____
2 _____   7 _____
3 _____   8 _____
4 _____   9 _____
5 _____   10 _____

Self-Image
Today, I am...

_____

_____

_____

Inspired Action
Today, I take these actions towards my goals...

1 _____   4 _____
2 _____   5 _____
3 _____   6 _____

Sending Love
Today, I send love to these people in my life...

1 _____

2 _____

3 _____

Powerful Positive Affirmation

I DESERVE ABUNDANCE AND PROSPERITY.

Gratitude
Today, I am so happy and grateful for...

1 _____   6 _____
2 _____   7 _____
3 _____   8 _____
4 _____   9 _____
5 _____   10 _____

Self-Image
Today, I am...

_____

_____

_____

Inspired Action
Today, I take these actions towards my goals...

1 _____   4 _____
2 _____   5 _____
3 _____   6 _____

Sending Love
Today, I send love to these people in my life...

1 _____
2 _____
3 _____

Powerful Positive Affirmation

EVERY DAY I'M GETTING HEALTHIER.

Gratitude
Today, I am so happy and grateful for...

1 _____   6 _____
2 _____   7 _____
3 _____   8 _____
4 _____   9 _____
5 _____   10 _____

Self-Image
Today, I am...

_____

_____

_____

Inspired Action
Today, I take these actions towards my goals...

1 _____   4 _____
2 _____   5 _____
3 _____   6 _____

Sending Love
Today, I send love to these people in my life...

1 _____
2 _____
3 _____

Powerful Positive Affirmation

I AM FULL OF VITALITY.

Gratitude

Today, I am so happy and grateful for...

1 _____   6 _____

2 _____   7 _____

3 _____   8 _____

4 _____   9 _____

5 _____   10 _____

Self-Image

Today, I am...

_____

_____

_____

Inspired Action

Today, I take these actions towards my goals...

1 _____   4 _____

2 _____   5 _____

3 _____   6 _____

Sending Love

Today, I send love to these people in my life...

1 _____

2 _____

3 _____

Powerful Positive Affirmation

I AM MY OWN SOURCE OF LOVE AND INSPIRATION.

Gratitude
Today, I am so happy and grateful for...

1 _____ 6 _____
2 _____ 7 _____
3 _____ 8 _____
4 _____ 9 _____
5 _____ 10 _____

Self-Image
Today, I am...

_____

_____

_____

Inspired Action
Today, I take these actions towards my goals...

1 _____ 4 _____
2 _____ 5 _____
3 _____ 6 _____

Sending Love
Today, I send love to these people in my life...

1 _____
2 _____
3 _____

Powerful Positive Affirmation

I HAVE AN ATTITUDE OF GRATITUDE.

Gratitude

Today, I am so happy and grateful for...

1 _____
2 _____
3 _____
4 _____
5 _____

6 _____
7 _____
8 _____
9 _____
10 _____

Self-Image

Today, I am...

_____

_____

_____

Inspired Action

Today, I take these actions towards my goals...

1 _____
2 _____
3 _____

4 _____
5 _____
6 _____

Sending Love

Today, I send love to these people in my life...

1 _____
2 _____
3 _____

Powerful Positive Affirmation

I AM SINCERELY GRATEFUL, AND THIS ATTRACTS POSITIVITY INTO MY LIFE.

Gratitude
Today, I am so happy and grateful for...

1 _____ 6 _____
2 _____ 7 _____
3 _____ 8 _____
4 _____ 9 _____
5 _____ 10 _____

Self-Image
Today, I am...

_____
_____
_____
_____

Inspired Action
Today, I take these actions towards my goals...

1 _____ 4 _____
2 _____ 5 _____
3 _____ 6 _____

Sending Love
Today, I send love to these people in my life...

1 _____
2 _____
3 _____

Powerful Positive Affirmation

I AM GRATEFUL FOR ALL OF THE POSITIVE THINGS THAT ARE COMING MY WAY.

Gratitude

Today, I am so happy and grateful for...

1 _____
2 _____
3 _____
4 _____
5 _____

6 _____
7 _____
8 _____
9 _____
10 _____

Self-Image

Today, I am...

_____

_____

_____

Inspired Action

Today, I take these actions towards my goals...

1 _____
2 _____
3 _____

4 _____
5 _____
6 _____

Sending Love

Today, I send love to these people in my life...

1 _____
2 _____
3 _____

Powerful Positive Affirmation

I GIVE MYSELF THE GIFT OF FREEDOM FROM THE PAST AND MOVE WITH JOY INTO THE NOW.

Gratitude

Today, I am so happy and grateful for...

1 _____   6 _____

2 _____   7 _____

3 _____   8 _____

4 _____   9 _____

5 _____   10 _____

Self-Image

Today, I am...

_____

_____

_____

Inspired Action

Today, I take these actions towards my goals...

1 _____   4 _____

2 _____   5 _____

3 _____   6 _____

Sending Love

Today, I send love to these people in my life...

1 _____

2 _____

3 _____

Powerful Positive Affirmation

I AM READY TO BE HEALED.
I AM WILLING TO FORGIVE.
ALL IS WELL.

Gratitude
Today, I am so happy and grateful for...

1 _____   6 _____

2 _____   7 _____

3 _____   8 _____

4 _____   9 _____

5 _____   10 _____

Self-Image
Today, I am...

_____

_____

_____

Inspired Action
Today, I take these actions towards my goals...

1 _____   4 _____

2 _____   5 _____

3 _____   6 _____

Sending Love
Today, I send love to these people in my life...

1 _____

2 _____

3 _____

Powerful Positive Affirmation

I TAKE GOOD CARE OF MY BODY
AND EAT A HEALTHY, WELL-BALANCED DIET.

Gratitude
Today, I am so happy and grateful for...

1 _____   6 _____
2 _____   7 _____
3 _____   8 _____
4 _____   9 _____
5 _____   10 _____

Self-Image
Today, I am...

_____
_____
_____

Inspired Action
Today, I take these actions towards my goals...

1 _____   4 _____
2 _____   5 _____
3 _____   6 _____

Sending Love
Today, I send love to these people in my life...

1 _____
2 _____
3 _____

Powerful Positive Affirmation

MY BODY IS A TEMPLE.
I KEEP IT CLEAN AND MAINTAIN ITS FUNCTIONALITY.

Gratitude
Today, I am so happy and grateful for...

1 _____   6 _____
2 _____   7 _____
3 _____   8 _____
4 _____   9 _____
5 _____   10 _____

Self-Image
Today, I am...

_____

_____

_____

Inspired Action
Today, I take these actions towards my goals...

1 _____   4 _____
2 _____   5 _____
3 _____   6 _____

Sending Love
Today, I send love to these people in my life...

1 _____

2 _____

3 _____

Powerful Positive Affirmation

I EXERCISE REGULARLY AND STRENGTHEN MY BODY.

Gratitude

Today, I am so happy and grateful for...

1 _____   6 _____

2 _____   7 _____

3 _____   8 _____

4 _____   9 _____

5 _____   10 _____

Self-Image

Today, I am...

_____

_____

_____

_____

Inspired Action

Today, I take these actions towards my goals...

1 _____   4 _____

2 _____   5 _____

3 _____   6 _____

Sending Love

Today, I send love to these people in my life...

1 _____

2 _____

3 _____

Powerful Positive Affirmation

MY TRUE, AUTHENTIC SELF GUIDES ALL MY ACTIONS.

Gratitude
Today, I am so happy and grateful for...

1 _____   6 _____
2 _____   7 _____
3 _____   8 _____
4 _____   9 _____
5 _____   10 _____

Self-Image
Today, I am...

_____

_____

_____

Inspired Action
Today, I take these actions towards my goals...

1 _____   4 _____
2 _____   5 _____
3 _____   6 _____

Sending Love
Today, I send love to these people in my life...

1 _____

2 _____

3 _____

Powerful Positive Affirmation

I AM A SPIRITUAL BEING THAT IS DIVINELY GUIDED.

Gratitude

Today, I am so happy and grateful for...

1 _____   6 _____

2 _____   7 _____

3 _____   8 _____

4 _____   9 _____

5 _____   10 _____

Self-Image

Today, I am...

_____

_____

_____

Inspired Action

Today, I take these actions towards my goals...

1 _____   4 _____

2 _____   5 _____

3 _____   6 _____

Sending Love

Today, I send love to these people in my life...

1 _____

2 _____

3 _____

Powerful Positive Affirmation

I AM IN ALIGNMENT WITH THE GOOD THAT I DESIRE.

Gratitude
Today, I am so happy and grateful for...

1 _____
2 _____
3 _____
4 _____
5 _____

6 _____
7 _____
8 _____
9 _____
10 _____

Self-Image
Today, I am...

_____

_____

_____

Inspired Action
Today, I take these actions towards my goals...

1 _____
2 _____
3 _____

4 _____
5 _____
6 _____

Sending Love
Today, I send love to these people in my life...

1 _____
2 _____
3 _____

Powerful Positive Affirmation

GRACE AND LOVE ARE WORKING THROUGH ME.

Day   Month   Year

Gratitude
Today, I am so happy and grateful for...

1 _____   6 _____
2 _____   7 _____
3 _____   8 _____
4 _____   9 _____
5 _____   10 _____

Self-Image
Today, I am...

_____
_____
_____

Inspired Action
Today, I take these actions towards my goals...

1 _____   4 _____
2 _____   5 _____
3 _____   6 _____

Sending Love
Today, I send love to these people in my life...

1 _____
2 _____
3 _____

Powerful Positive Affirmation

I SEE THE SPARK OF DIVINITY
IN MYSELF AND IN OTHERS.

Gratitude

Today, I am so happy and grateful for...

1 _____   6 _____
2 _____   7 _____
3 _____   8 _____
4 _____   9 _____
5 _____   10 _____

Self-Image

Today, I am...

_____

_____

_____

Inspired Action

Today, I take these actions towards my goals...

1 _____   4 _____
2 _____   5 _____
3 _____   6 _____

Sending Love

Today, I send love to these people in my life...

1 _____

2 _____

3 _____

Powerful Positive Affirmation

EVERYTHING LEADS TO SOMETHING BETTER.

Gratitude
Today, I am so happy and grateful for...

1 _____ 6 _____

2 _____ 7 _____

3 _____ 8 _____

4 _____ 9 _____

5 _____ 10 _____

Self-Image
Today, I am...

_____

_____

_____

Inspired Action
Today, I take these actions towards my goals...

1 _____ 4 _____

2 _____ 5 _____

3 _____ 6 _____

Sending Love
Today, I send love to these people in my life...

1 _____

2 _____

3 _____

Powerful Positive Affirmation

I FIND POSITIVITY IN EVERY SITUATION.

Gratitude

Today, I am so happy and grateful for...

1 _____ 6 _____

2 _____ 7 _____

3 _____ 8 _____

4 _____ 9 _____

5 _____ 10 _____

Self-Image
Today, I am...

_____

_____

_____

Inspired Action
Today, I take these actions towards my goals...

1 _____ 4 _____

2 _____ 5 _____

3 _____ 6 _____

Sending Love
Today, I send love to these people in my life...

1 _____

2 _____

3 _____

Powerful Positive Affirmation

I AM ABLE TO FIND OPTIMISTIC WAYS OF DEALING WITH EVERYTHING.

Gratitude

Today, I am so happy and grateful for...

1 _____
2 _____
3 _____
4 _____
5 _____

6 _____
7 _____
8 _____
9 _____
10 _____

Self-Image

Today, I am...

_____

_____

_____

Inspired Action

Today, I take these actions towards my goals...

1 _____
2 _____
3 _____

4 _____
5 _____
6 _____

Sending Love

Today, I send love to these people in my life...

1 _____

2 _____

3 _____

Powerful Positive Affirmation

THERE IS GOOD TO BE FOUND IN EVERY SITUATION, EVEN IF I MAY NOT SEE IT AT THE MOMENT.

Gratitude

Today, I am so happy and grateful for...

1 _____   6 _____

2 _____   7 _____

3 _____   8 _____

4 _____   9 _____

5 _____   10 _____

Self-Image

Today, I am...

_____

_____

_____

Inspired Action

Today, I take these actions towards my goals...

1 _____   4 _____

2 _____   5 _____

3 _____   6 _____

Sending Love

Today, I send love to these people in my life...

1 _____

2 _____

3 _____

Powerful Positive Affirmation

THERE IS ALWAYS A WAY.
THERE IS ALWAYS A SOLUTION.

Gratitude

Today, I am so happy and grateful for...

1 _____   6 _____
2 _____   7 _____
3 _____   8 _____
4 _____   9 _____
5 _____   10 _____

Self-Image
Today, I am...

_____
_____
_____

Inspired Action
Today, I take these actions towards my goals...

1 _____   4 _____
2 _____   5 _____
3 _____   6 _____

Sending Love
Today, I send love to these people in my life...

1 _____
2 _____
3 _____

Powerful Positive Affirmation

MY INTUITION AND INNER WISDOM GUIDE ME IN EVERY SITUATION.

Gratitude
Today, I am so happy and grateful for...

1 _____   6 _____

2 _____   7 _____

3 _____   8 _____

4 _____   9 _____

5 _____   10 _____

Self-Image
Today, I am...

_____

_____

_____

Inspired Action
Today, I take these actions towards my goals...

1 _____   4 _____

2 _____   5 _____

3 _____   6 _____

Sending Love
Today, I send love to these people in my life...

1 _____

2 _____

3 _____

Powerful Positive Affirmation

LIFE ALWAYS WANTS THE BEST FOR ME.

Gratitude
Today, I am so happy and grateful for...

1 _____   6 _____

2 _____   7 _____

3 _____   8 _____

4 _____   9 _____

5 _____   10 _____

Self-Image
Today, I am...

_____

_____

_____

Inspired Action
Today, I take these actions towards my goals...

1 _____   4 _____

2 _____   5 _____

3 _____   6 _____

Sending Love
Today, I send love to these people in my life...

1 _____

2 _____

3 _____

Powerful Positive Affirmation

LIFE IS ABUNDANT WITH OPPORTUNITIES.

Gratitude
Today, I am so happy and grateful for...

1 _____   6 _____
2 _____   7 _____
3 _____   8 _____
4 _____   9 _____
5 _____   10 _____

Self-Image
Today, I am...

_____
_____
_____

Inspired Action
Today, I take these actions towards my goals...

1 _____   4 _____
2 _____   5 _____
3 _____   6 _____

Sending Love
Today, I send love to these people in my life...

1 _____
2 _____
3 _____

Powerful Positive Affirmation

EVERY SITUATION SERVES MY HIGHEST GOOD.

Gratitude

Today, I am so happy and grateful for...

1 _____   6 _____

2 _____   7 _____

3 _____   8 _____

4 _____   9 _____

5 _____   10 _____

Self-Image

Today, I am...

_____

_____

_____

Inspired Action

Today, I take these actions towards my goals...

1 _____   4 _____

2 _____   5 _____

3 _____   6 _____

Sending Love

Today, I send love to these people in my life...

1 _____

2 _____

3 _____

Powerful Positive Affirmation

I AM A KIND AND UNIQUE PERSON.
I HAVE A LOT TO OFFER IN A FRIENDSHIP.

Gratitude

Today, I am so happy and grateful for...

1 _____   6 _____

2 _____   7 _____

3 _____   8 _____

4 _____   9 _____

5 _____   10 _____

Self-Image

Today, I am...

_____

_____

_____

Inspired Action

Today, I take these actions towards my goals...

1 _____   4 _____

2 _____   5 _____

3 _____   6 _____

Sending Love

Today, I send love to these people in my life...

1 _____

2 _____

3 _____

Powerful Positive Affirmation

I ENJOY MY OWN COMPANY.
IT HELPS ME TO GET IN TOUCH WITH MY TRUE SELF.

Gratitude
Today, I am so happy and grateful for...

1 _____   6 _____

2 _____   7 _____

3 _____   8 _____

4 _____   9 _____

5 _____   10 _____

Self-Image
Today, I am...

_____

_____

_____

Inspired Action
Today, I take these actions towards my goals...

1 _____   4 _____

2 _____   5 _____

3 _____   6 _____

Sending Love
Today, I send love to these people in my life...

1 _____

2 _____

3 _____

Powerful Positive Affirmation

I AM AT PEACE AND HAPPY.

Gratitude

Today, I am so happy and grateful for...

1 _____   6 _____
2 _____   7 _____
3 _____   8 _____
4 _____   9 _____
5 _____   10 _____

Self-Image

Today, I am...

_____

_____

_____

Inspired Action

Today, I take these actions towards my goals...

1 _____   4 _____
2 _____   5 _____
3 _____   6 _____

Sending Love

Today, I send love to these people in my life...

1 _____
2 _____
3 _____

Powerful Positive Affirmation

I CAN ALWAYS BRIGHTEN ANOTHER PERSON'S DAY BY DOING SOMETHING WITH THEM.

Gratitude

Today, I am so happy and grateful for...

1 _____   6 _____
2 _____   7 _____
3 _____   8 _____
4 _____   9 _____
5 _____   10 _____

Self-Image

Today, I am...

_____

_____

_____

Inspired Action

Today, I take these actions towards my goals...

1 _____   4 _____
2 _____   5 _____
3 _____   6 _____

Sending Love

Today, I send love to these people in my life...

1 _____
2 _____
3 _____

Powerful Positive Affirmation

MY INTUITION AND WISDOM
GUIDE ME IN THE RIGHT DIRECTION.

Gratitude
Today, I am so happy and grateful for...

1 _____   6 _____

2 _____   7 _____

3 _____   8 _____

4 _____   9 _____

5 _____   10 _____

Self-Image
Today, I am...

_____

_____

_____

Inspired Action
Today, I take these actions towards my goals...

1 _____   4 _____

2 _____   5 _____

3 _____   6 _____

Sending Love
Today, I send love to these people in my life...

1 _____

2 _____

3 _____

Powerful Positive Affirmation

I LOVE MY LIFE.

Gratitude

Today, I am so happy and grateful for...

1 _____   6 _____
2 _____   7 _____
3 _____   8 _____
4 _____   9 _____
5 _____   10 _____

Self-Image

Today, I am...

_____

_____

_____

Inspired Action

Today, I take these actions towards my goals...

1 _____   4 _____
2 _____   5 _____
3 _____   6 _____

Sending Love

Today, I send love to these people in my life...

1 _____
2 _____
3 _____

Powerful Positive Affirmation

MY FRIENDSHIPS ARE MEANINGFUL, SUPPORTIVE AND REWARDING.

Gratitude
Today, I am so happy and grateful for...

1 _____
2 _____
3 _____
4 _____
5 _____

6 _____
7 _____
8 _____
9 _____
10 _____

Self-Image
Today, I am...

_____

_____

_____

Inspired Action
Today, I take these actions towards my goals...

1 _____
2 _____
3 _____

4 _____
5 _____
6 _____

Sending Love
Today, I send love to these people in my life...

1 _____
2 _____
3 _____

Powerful Positive Affirmation

I AM ACCEPTING OF OTHERS; IT HELPS ME TO ESTABLISH LONG-LASTING FRIENDSHIPS.

Gratitude

Today, I am so happy and grateful for...

1 _____   6 _____

2 _____   7 _____

3 _____   8 _____

4 _____   9 _____

5 _____   10 _____

Self-Image

Today, I am...

_____

_____

_____

Inspired Action

Today, I take these actions towards my goals...

1 _____   4 _____

2 _____   5 _____

3 _____   6 _____

Sending Love

Today, I send love to these people in my life...

1 _____

2 _____

3 _____

Powerful Positive Affirmation

TODAY WILL BE A FABULOUS DAY!

Gratitude

Today, I am so happy and grateful for...

1 _____   6 _____
2 _____   7 _____
3 _____   8 _____
4 _____   9 _____
5 _____   10 _____

Self-Image
Today, I am...

_____

_____

_____

Inspired Action
Today, I take these actions towards my goals...

1 _____   4 _____
2 _____   5 _____
3 _____   6 _____

Sending Love
Today, I send love to these people in my life...

1 _____

2 _____

3 _____

Powerful Positive Affirmation

THIS DAY WILL BRING ME JOY, FULFILLMENT AND HAPPINESS.

Day   Month   Year

Gratitude
Today, I am so happy and grateful for...

1 _____ 6 _____
2 _____ 7 _____
3 _____ 8 _____
4 _____ 9 _____
5 _____ 10 _____

Self-Image
Today, I am...

_____
_____
_____

Inspired Action
Today, I take these actions towards my goals...

1 _____ 4 _____
2 _____ 5 _____
3 _____ 6 _____

Sending Love
Today, I send love to these people in my life...

1 _____
2 _____
3 _____

Powerful Positive Affirmation

I AM EXCITED TO SEE WHAT THE PRESENT DAY HOLDS.

Gratitude
Today, I am so happy and grateful for...

Day   Month   Year

1 _____   6 _____

2 _____   7 _____

3 _____   8 _____

4 _____   9 _____

5 _____   10 _____

Self-Image
Today, I am...

_____

_____

_____

Inspired Action
Today, I take these actions towards my goals...

1 _____   4 _____

2 _____   5 _____

3 _____   6 _____

Sending Love
Today, I send love to these people in my life...

1 _____

2 _____

3 _____

Powerful Positive Affirmation

I AM OPTIMISTIC ABOUT THE FUTURE.

Gratitude

Today, I am so happy and grateful for...

1 _____ 6 _____

2 _____ 7 _____

3 _____ 8 _____

4 _____ 9 _____

5 _____ 10 _____

Self-Image

Today, I am...

_____

_____

_____

Inspired Action

Today, I take these actions towards my goals...

1 _____ 4 _____

2 _____ 5 _____

3 _____ 6 _____

Sending Love

Today, I send love to these people in my life...

1 _____

2 _____

3 _____

Powerful Positive Affirmation

I HAVE THE POWER TO MAKE TODAY AMAZING!

Gratitude

Today, I am so happy and grateful for...

1 _____
2 _____
3 _____
4 _____
5 _____

6 _____
7 _____
8 _____
9 _____
10 _____

Self-Image

Today, I am...

_____

_____

_____

Inspired Action

Today, I take these actions towards my goals...

1 _____
2 _____
3 _____

4 _____
5 _____
6 _____

Sending Love

Today, I send love to these people in my life...

1 _____
2 _____
3 _____

Powerful Positive Affirmation

I BELIEVE IN MY ABILITY TO GAIN VALUABLE INSIGHTS FROM THIS SITUATION.

Gratitude

Today, I am so happy and grateful for...

1 _____   6 _____

2 _____   7 _____

3 _____   8 _____

4 _____   9 _____

5 _____   10 _____

Self-Image

Today, I am...

_____

_____

_____

Inspired Action

Today, I take these actions towards my goals...

1 _____   4 _____

2 _____   5 _____

3 _____   6 _____

Sending Love

Today, I send love to these people in my life...

1 _____

2 _____

3 _____

Powerful Positive Affirmation

I AM UNIQUE, SO I WILL BE UNIQUELY SUCCESSFUL.

Gratitude
Today, I am so happy and grateful for...

1 _____   6 _____
2 _____   7 _____
3 _____   8 _____
4 _____   9 _____
5 _____   10 _____

Self-Image
Today, I am...

_____
_____
_____

Inspired Action
Today, I take these actions towards my goals...

1 _____   4 _____
2 _____   5 _____
3 _____   6 _____

Sending Love
Today, I send love to these people in my life...

1 _____
2 _____
3 _____

Powerful Positive Affirmation

I BELIEVE IN MY LIMITLESS POTENTIAL.

Gratitude
Today, I am so happy and grateful for...

1 _____   6 _____
2 _____   7 _____
3 _____   8 _____
4 _____   9 _____
5 _____   10 _____

Self-Image
Today, I am...

_____
_____
_____

Inspired Action
Today, I take these actions towards my goals...

1 _____   4 _____
2 _____   5 _____
3 _____   6 _____

Sending Love
Today, I send love to these people in my life...

1 _____
2 _____
3 _____

Powerful Positive Affirmation

I HAVE ALL THE POWER, SKILL AND INSPIRATION TO ACHIEVE MY DREAMS.

Gratitude
Today, I am so happy and grateful for...

1 _____   6 _____
2 _____   7 _____
3 _____   8 _____
4 _____   9 _____
5 _____   10 _____

Self-Image
Today, I am...

_____

_____

_____

Inspired Action
Today, I take these actions towards my goals...

1 _____   4 _____
2 _____   5 _____
3 _____   6 _____

Sending Love
Today, I send love to these people in my life...

1 _____
2 _____
3 _____

Powerful Positive Affirmation

I AM SUCCESSFUL IN WHATEVER I DO.

Gratitude

Today, I am so happy and grateful for...

1 _____   6 _____

2 _____   7 _____

3 _____   8 _____

4 _____   9 _____

5 _____   10 _____

Self-Image

Today, I am...

_____

_____

_____

Inspired Action

Today, I take these actions towards my goals...

1 _____   4 _____

2 _____   5 _____

3 _____   6 _____

Sending Love

Today, I send love to these people in my life...

1 _____

2 _____

3 _____

Powerful Positive Affirmation

I ATTRACT SUCCESS.

Gratitude

Today, I am so happy and grateful for...

1 _____   6 _____

2 _____   7 _____

3 _____   8 _____

4 _____   9 _____

5 _____   10 _____

Self-Image

Today, I am...

_____

_____

_____

Inspired Action

Today, I take these actions towards my goals...

1 _____   4 _____

2 _____   5 _____

3 _____   6 _____

Sending Love

Today, I send love to these people in my life...

1 _____

2 _____

3 _____

Powerful Positive Affirmation

I TRUST MYSELF AND MY INTUITION, ABOVE ANYONE ELSE.

Gratitude

Today, I am so happy and grateful for...

1 _____   6 _____

2 _____   7 _____

3 _____   8 _____

4 _____   9 _____

5 _____   10 _____

Self-Image

Today, I am...

_____

_____

_____

Inspired Action

Today, I take these actions towards my goals...

1 _____   4 _____

2 _____   5 _____

3 _____   6 _____

Sending Love

Today, I send love to these people in my life...

1 _____

2 _____

3 _____

Powerful Positive Affirmation

TO LOVE MYSELF IS THE ULTIMATE LOVE.

Gratitude
Today, I am so happy and grateful for...

1 _____   6 _____

2 _____   7 _____

3 _____   8 _____

4 _____   9 _____

5 _____   10 _____

Self-Image
Today, I am...

_____

_____

_____

Inspired Action
Today, I take these actions towards my goals...

1 _____   4 _____

2 _____   5 _____

3 _____   6 _____

Sending Love
Today, I send love to these people in my life...

1 _____

2 _____

3 _____

Powerful Positive Affirmation

I KNOW MY CALLING AND THE WORK
I AM SUPPOSED TO DO IN MY LIFE.

Gratitude
Today, I am so happy and grateful for...

1 _____   6 _____
2 _____   7 _____
3 _____   8 _____
4 _____   9 _____
5 _____   10 _____

Self-Image
Today, I am...

_____
_____
_____
_____

Inspired Action
Today, I take these actions towards my goals...

1 _____   4 _____
2 _____   5 _____
3 _____   6 _____

Sending Love
Today, I send love to these people in my life...

1 _____
2 _____
3 _____

Powerful Positive Affirmation

I AM PURSUING MY OWN DEFINITION OF SUCCESS.

◆ ◦ ◆ ◦ ◆ ◦ ◆ ◦ ◉

Gratitude

Today, I am so happy and grateful for...

1 _____   6 _____

2 _____   7 _____

3 _____   8 _____

4 _____   9 _____

5 _____   10 _____

Self-Image

Today, I am...

_____

_____

_____

Inspired Action

Today, I take these actions towards my goals...

1 _____   4 _____

2 _____   5 _____

3 _____   6 _____

Sending Love

Today, I send love to these people in my life...

1 _____

2 _____

3 _____

Powerful Positive Affirmation

I GET BETTER WITH EACH DAY.
PRACTICE HELPS ME TO ATTAIN GREATNESS.

Gratitude

Today, I am so happy and grateful for...

1 _____
2 _____
3 _____
4 _____
5 _____

6 _____
7 _____
8 _____
9 _____
10 _____

Self-Image

Today, I am...

_____

_____

_____

Inspired Action

Today, I take these actions towards my goals...

1 _____
2 _____
3 _____

4 _____
5 _____
6 _____

Sending Love

Today, I send love to these people in my life...

1 _____
2 _____
3 _____

Powerful Positive Affirmation

I ALWAYS GIVE MY BEST AND AM A GOOD-HEARTED PERSON.

Gratitude
Today, I am so happy and grateful for...

1 _____   6 _____

2 _____   7 _____

3 _____   8 _____

4 _____   9 _____

5 _____   10 _____

Self-Image
Today, I am...

_____

_____

_____

Inspired Action
Today, I take these actions towards my goals...

1 _____   4 _____

2 _____   5 _____

3 _____   6 _____

Sending Love
Today, I send love to these people in my life...

1 _____

2 _____

3 _____

Powerful Positive Affirmation

I KNOW THAT MY THOUGHTS BECOME THINGS.

Gratitude
Today, I am so happy and grateful for...

1 _____   6 _____
2 _____   7 _____
3 _____   8 _____
4 _____   9 _____
5 _____   10 _____

Self-Image
Today, I am...

_____
_____
_____

Inspired Action
Today, I take these actions towards my goals...

1 _____   4 _____
2 _____   5 _____
3 _____   6 _____

Sending Love
Today, I send love to these people in my life...

1 _____
2 _____
3 _____

Powerful Positive Affirmation

EVERY DAY, I ENHANCE AND DEVELOP MY SELF-IMAGE AND BE THE AMAZING, INCREDIBLE PERSON I KNOW I AM.

Gratitude
Today, I am so happy and grateful for...

1 _____   6 _____
2 _____   7 _____
3 _____   8 _____
4 _____   9 _____
5 _____   10 _____

Self-Image
Today, I am...

_____

_____

_____

Inspired Action
Today, I take these actions towards my goals...

1 _____   4 _____
2 _____   5 _____
3 _____   6 _____

Sending Love
Today, I send love to these people in my life...

1 _____
2 _____
3 _____

Powerful Positive Affirmation

AMAZING IDEAS ARE USING ME TO CREATE THE LIFE OF MY DREAMS.

Gratitude

Today, I am so happy and grateful for...

1 _____   6 _____
2 _____   7 _____
3 _____   8 _____
4 _____   9 _____
5 _____   10 _____

Self-Image
Today, I am...

_____

_____

_____

Inspired Action
Today, I take these actions towards my goals...

1 _____   4 _____
2 _____   5 _____
3 _____   6 _____

Sending Love
Today, I send love to these people in my life...

1 _____

2 _____

3 _____

Powerful Positive Affirmation

MY MARVELOUS IMAGINATION KEEPS MY MIND OPEN TO NEW OPPORTUNITIES, LOVE AND SUCCESS.

Gratitude
Today, I am so happy and grateful for...

1 _____   6 _____
2 _____   7 _____
3 _____   8 _____
4 _____   9 _____
5 _____   10 _____

Self-Image
Today, I am...

_____

_____

_____

Inspired Action
Today, I take these actions towards my goals...

1 _____   4 _____
2 _____   5 _____
3 _____   6 _____

Sending Love
Today, I send love to these people in my life...

1 _____
2 _____
3 _____

Powerful Positive Affirmation

MY AWARENESS IS EXPANDING EACH DAY.

Gratitude

Today, I am so happy and grateful for...

1 _____   6 _____

2 _____   7 _____

3 _____   8 _____

4 _____   9 _____

5 _____   10 _____

Self-Image

Today, I am...

_____

_____

_____

Inspired Action

Today, I take these actions towards my goals...

1 _____   4 _____

2 _____   5 _____

3 _____   6 _____

Sending Love

Today, I send love to these people in my life...

1 _____

2 _____

3 _____

Powerful Positive Affirmation

EVERYTHING I NEED IS RIGHT HERE. RIGHT NOW.

Gratitude
Today, I am so happy and grateful for...

1 _____
2 _____
3 _____
4 _____
5 _____

6 _____
7 _____
8 _____
9 _____
10 _____

Self-Image
Today, I am...

_____

_____

_____

Inspired Action
Today, I take these actions towards my goals...

1 _____
2 _____
3 _____

4 _____
5 _____
6 _____

Sending Love
Today, I send love to these people in my life...

1 _____
2 _____
3 _____

Powerful Positive Affirmation

I MAKE A HABIT OF EXPANDING MY MIND TO DO NEW THINGS TO TAKE MY MIND TO NEW HEIGHTS.

Gratitude
Today, I am so happy and grateful for...

1 _____
2 _____
3 _____
4 _____
5 _____

6 _____
7 _____
8 _____
9 _____
10 _____

Self-Image
Today, I am...

_____
_____
_____

Inspired Action
Today, I take these actions towards my goals...

1 _____
2 _____
3 _____

4 _____
5 _____
6 _____

Sending Love
Today, I send love to these people in my life...

1 _____
2 _____
3 _____

Powerful Positive Affirmation

I ATTRACT POSITIVE PEOPLE WITH WHOM I QUICKLY MAKE FRIENDS.

Gratitude

Today, I am so happy and grateful for...

1 _____ 6 _____

2 _____ 7 _____

3 _____ 8 _____

4 _____ 9 _____

5 _____ 10 _____

Self-Image

Today, I am...

_____

_____

_____

Inspired Action

Today, I take these actions towards my goals...

1 _____ 4 _____

2 _____ 5 _____

3 _____ 6 _____

Sending Love

Today, I send love to these people in my life...

1 _____

2 _____

3 _____

Powerful Positive Affirmation

I FEEL RELAXED AND COMFORTABLE AROUND OTHER PEOPLE.

Gratitude
Today, I am so happy and grateful for...

1 _____
2 _____
3 _____
4 _____
5 _____

6 _____
7 _____
8 _____
9 _____
10 _____

Self-Image
Today, I am...

_____
_____
_____
_____

Inspired Action
Today, I take these actions towards my goals...

1 _____
2 _____
3 _____

4 _____
5 _____
6 _____

Sending Love
Today, I send love to these people in my life...

1 _____
2 _____
3 _____

Powerful Positive Affirmation

I CHOOSE TO LEARN, UNLEARN AND RELEARN TO CREATE THE LIFE I WANT.

Gratitude

Today, I am so happy and grateful for...

1 _____   6 _____

2 _____   7 _____

3 _____   8 _____

4 _____   9 _____

5 _____   10 _____

Self-Image

Today, I am...

_____

_____

_____

Inspired Action

Today, I take these actions towards my goals...

1 _____   4 _____

2 _____   5 _____

3 _____   6 _____

Sending Love

Today, I send love to these people in my life...

1 _____

2 _____

3 _____

Powerful Positive Affirmation

I HAVE THE POWER TO CREATE THE VISION I WANT.

Gratitude
Today, I am so happy and grateful for...

1 _____   6 _____
2 _____   7 _____
3 _____   8 _____
4 _____   9 _____
5 _____   10 _____

Self-Image
Today, I am...

_____

_____

_____

Inspired Action
Today, I take these actions towards my goals...

1 _____   4 _____
2 _____   5 _____
3 _____   6 _____

Sending Love
Today, I send love to these people in my life...

1 _____
2 _____
3 _____

Powerful Positive Affirmation

I AM IN TOUCH WITH MY HEART'S DESIRE, AND I KNOW I HAVE THE POWER TO MAKE IT REAL.

Gratitude
Today, I am so happy and grateful for...

1 _____   6 _____
2 _____   7 _____
3 _____   8 _____
4 _____   9 _____
5 _____   10 _____

Self-Image
Today, I am...

_____

_____

_____

Inspired Action
Today, I take these actions towards my goals...

1 _____   4 _____
2 _____   5 _____
3 _____   6 _____

Sending Love
Today, I send love to these people in my life...

1 _____
2 _____
3 _____

Powerful Positive Affirmation

I AM LIVING FROM MY HIGHEST SELF.

Gratitude
Today, I am so happy and grateful for...

1 _____   6 _____
2 _____   7 _____
3 _____   8 _____
4 _____   9 _____
5 _____   10 _____

Self-Image
Today, I am...

_____

_____

_____

Inspired Action
Today, I take these actions towards my goals...

1 _____   4 _____
2 _____   5 _____
3 _____   6 _____

Sending Love
Today, I send love to these people in my life...

1 _____
2 _____
3 _____

Powerful Positive Affirmation

THINGS ARE FALLING PERFECTLY
INTO PLACE FOR ME.

Gratitude

Today, I am so happy and grateful for...

1 _____
2 _____
3 _____
4 _____
5 _____

6 _____
7 _____
8 _____
9 _____
10 _____

Self-Image

Today, I am...

_____

_____

_____

Inspired Action

Today, I take these actions towards my goals...

1 _____
2 _____
3 _____

4 _____
5 _____
6 _____

Sending Love

Today, I send love to these people in my life...

1 _____
2 _____
3 _____

Powerful Positive Affirmation

I AM FULL OF GRATITUDE AND SO, CONTINUE TO ATTRACT INCREDIBLE OPPORTUNITIES.

Gratitude
Today, I am so happy and grateful for...

Day   Month   Year

1 _____   6 _____
2 _____   7 _____
3 _____   8 _____
4 _____   9 _____
5 _____   10 _____

Self-Image
Today, I am...

_____
_____
_____

Inspired Action
Today, I take these actions towards my goals...

1 _____   4 _____
2 _____   5 _____
3 _____   6 _____

Sending Love
Today, I send love to these people in my life...

1 _____
2 _____
3 _____

Powerful Positive Affirmation

I LOVE ME, AND I THE LIFE I AM CREATING.

Gratitude

Today, I am so happy and grateful for...

1 _____   6 _____

2 _____   7 _____

3 _____   8 _____

4 _____   9 _____

5 _____   10 _____

Self-Image
Today, I am...

_____

_____

_____

Inspired Action
Today, I take these actions towards my goals...

1 _____   4 _____

2 _____   5 _____

3 _____   6 _____

Sending Love
Today, I send love to these people in my life...

1 _____

2 _____

3 _____

Powerful Positive Affirmation

WHATEVER I WANT CAN FLOW TO ME.

Gratitude

Today, I am so happy and grateful for...

1 _____   6 _____

2 _____   7 _____

3 _____   8 _____

4 _____   9 _____

5 _____   10 _____

Self-Image
Today, I am...

_____

_____

_____

Inspired Action
Today, I take these actions towards my goals...

1 _____   4 _____

2 _____   5 _____

3 _____   6 _____

Sending Love
Today, I send love to these people in my life...

1 _____

2 _____

3 _____

Powerful Positive Affirmation

MY RELATIONSHIP WITH MY INNER BEING IS MY STRONGEST PARTNERSHIP.

Gratitude
Today, I am so happy and grateful for...

1 _____   6 _____

2 _____   7 _____

3 _____   8 _____

4 _____   9 _____

5 _____   10 _____

Self-Image
Today, I am...

_____

_____

_____

Inspired Action
Today, I take these actions towards my goals...

1 _____   4 _____

2 _____   5 _____

3 _____   6 _____

Sending Love
Today, I send love to these people in my life...

1 _____

2 _____

3 _____

Powerful Positive Affirmation

NO MATTER WHERE I AM, I HAVE THE ABILITY TO FOCUS IN A WAY THAT IS PLEASING TO ME.

Gratitude

Today, I am so happy and grateful for...

1 _____ 6 _____

2 _____ 7 _____

3 _____ 8 _____

4 _____ 9 _____

5 _____ 10 _____

Self-Image

Today, I am...

_____

_____

_____

Inspired Action

Today, I take these actions towards my goals...

1 _____ 4 _____

2 _____ 5 _____

3 _____ 6 _____

Sending Love

Today, I send love to these people in my life...

1 _____

2 _____

3 _____

Powerful Positive Affirmation

I'M DOING GOOD, AND IT'S GETTING BETTER!

Gratitude
Today, I am so happy and grateful for...

1 _____
2 _____
3 _____
4 _____
5 _____

6 _____
7 _____
8 _____
9 _____
10 _____

Self-Image
Today, I am...

_____
_____
_____

Inspired Action
Today, I take these actions towards my goals...

1 _____
2 _____
3 _____

4 _____
5 _____
6 _____

Sending Love
Today, I send love to these people in my life...

1 _____
2 _____
3 _____

Powerful Positive Affirmation

I TRUST THAT I'M FIGURING THIS OUT.

Gratitude
Today, I am so happy and grateful for...

1 _____   6 _____
2 _____   7 _____
3 _____   8 _____
4 _____   9 _____
5 _____   10 _____

Self-Image
Today, I am...

_____

_____

_____

Inspired Action
Today, I take these actions towards my goals...

1 _____   4 _____
2 _____   5 _____
3 _____   6 _____

Sending Love
Today, I send love to these people in my life...

1 _____
2 _____
3 _____

Powerful Positive Affirmation

NOTHING OTHER THAN FEELING GOOD WILL DO FOR ME.

Gratitude

Today, I am so happy and grateful for...

1 _____   6 _____

2 _____   7 _____

3 _____   8 _____

4 _____   9 _____

5 _____   10 _____

Self-Image

Today, I am...

_____

_____

_____

Inspired Action

Today, I take these actions towards my goals...

1 _____   4 _____

2 _____   5 _____

3 _____   6 _____

Sending Love

Today, I send love to these people in my life...

1 _____

2 _____

3 _____

Powerful Positive Affirmation

I LOVE BEING THE CLEAR EXAMPLE THAT I AM. I LOVE OFFERING MY VIBRATION DELIBERATELY, AND I LOVE WATCHING ALL THE UNIVERSAL FACTORS LINING THINGS UP.

Gratitude
Today, I am so happy and grateful for...

1 _____   6 _____
2 _____   7 _____
3 _____   8 _____
4 _____   9 _____
5 _____   10 _____

Self-Image
Today, I am...

_____
_____
_____

Inspired Action
Today, I take these actions towards my goals...

1 _____   4 _____
2 _____   5 _____
3 _____   6 _____

Sending Love
Today, I send love to these people in my life...

1 _____
2 _____
3 _____

Powerful Positive Affirmation

IT IS MY DOMINANT INTENTION TO FEEL
THE WAY I WANT TO FEEL.

Gratitude

Today, I am so happy and grateful for...

1 _____   6 _____
2 _____   7 _____
3 _____   8 _____
4 _____   9 _____
5 _____   10 _____

Self-Image

Today, I am...

_____

_____

_____

Inspired Action

Today, I take these actions towards my goals...

1 _____   4 _____
2 _____   5 _____
3 _____   6 _____

Sending Love

Today, I send love to these people in my life...

1 _____
2 _____
3 _____

Powerful Positive Affirmation

I WANT IT, AND I EXPECT THE GOOD I DESIRE TO COME TO ME.

Gratitude
Today, I am so happy and grateful for...

1 _____ 6 _____

2 _____ 7 _____

3 _____ 8 _____

4 _____ 9 _____

5 _____ 10 _____

Self-Image
Today, I am...

_____

_____

_____

Inspired Action
Today, I take these actions towards my goals...

1 _____ 4 _____

2 _____ 5 _____

3 _____ 6 _____

Sending Love
Today, I send love to these people in my life...

1 _____

2 _____

3 _____

Powerful Positive Affirmation

FEELING BETTER IS THE MANIFESTATION I AM REACHING FOR.

Gratitude

Today, I am so happy and grateful for...

1 _____ 6 _____
2 _____ 7 _____
3 _____ 8 _____
4 _____ 9 _____
5 _____ 10 _____

Self-Image

Today, I am...

_____

_____

_____

Inspired Action

Today, I take these actions towards my goals...

1 _____ 4 _____
2 _____ 5 _____
3 _____ 6 _____

Sending Love

Today, I send love to these people in my life...

1 _____
2 _____
3 _____

Powerful Positive Affirmation

I AM TO LIVE HAPPILY EVER AFTER.

Gratitude

Today, I am so happy and grateful for...

1 _____
2 _____
3 _____
4 _____
5 _____

6 _____
7 _____
8 _____
9 _____
10 _____

Self-Image

Today, I am...

_____
_____
_____

Inspired Action

Today, I take these actions towards my goals...

1 _____
2 _____
3 _____

4 _____
5 _____
6 _____

Sending Love

Today, I send love to these people in my life...

1 _____
2 _____
3 _____

Powerful Positive Affirmation

I AM THE ONLY ONE RESPONSIBLE FOR HOW I FEEL.

Gratitude
Today, I am so happy and grateful for...

1 _____   6 _____

2 _____   7 _____

3 _____   8 _____

4 _____   9 _____

5 _____   10 _____

Self-Image
Today, I am...

_____

_____

_____

Inspired Action
Today, I take these actions towards my goals...

1 _____   4 _____

2 _____   5 _____

3 _____   6 _____

Sending Love
Today, I send love to these people in my life...

1 _____

2 _____

3 _____

Powerful Positive Affirmation

I'M ENJOYING THE JOURNEY BECAUSE THE DESTINATION IS CERTAIN.

Gratitude

Today, I am so happy and grateful for...

1 _____   6 _____

2 _____   7 _____

3 _____   8 _____

4 _____   9 _____

5 _____   10 _____

Self-Image

Today, I am...

_____

_____

_____

Inspired Action

Today, I take these actions towards my goals...

1 _____   4 _____

2 _____   5 _____

3 _____   6 _____

Sending Love

Today, I send love to these people in my life...

1 _____

2 _____

3 _____

Powerful Positive Affirmation

RIGHT NOW, I AM GOING TO FIND
THE BEST-FEELING THOUGHT THAT I CAN.

Gratitude
Today, I am so happy and grateful for...

1 _____ 6 _____

2 _____ 7 _____

3 _____ 8 _____

4 _____ 9 _____

5 _____ 10 _____

Self-Image
Today, I am...

_____

_____

_____

Inspired Action
Today, I take these actions towards my goals...

1 _____ 4 _____

2 _____ 5 _____

3 _____ 6 _____

Sending Love
Today, I send love to these people in my life...

1 _____

2 _____

3 _____

Powerful Positive Affirmation

I KNOW I'M GOOD AT WHAT I DO.
I KNOW THAT I ALWAYS FIGURE THINGS OUT.
I KNOW THAT THINGS DO WORK OUT FOR ME.

Gratitude
Today, I am so happy and grateful for...

1 _____   6 _____
2 _____   7 _____
3 _____   8 _____
4 _____   9 _____
5 _____   10 _____

Self-Image
Today, I am...

_____

_____

_____

Inspired Action
Today, I take these actions towards my goals...

1 _____   4 _____
2 _____   5 _____
3 _____   6 _____

Sending Love
Today, I send love to these people in my life...

1 _____

2 _____

3 _____

Powerful Positive Affirmation

THE HAPPIER I AM, THE BETTER THINGS GET.

Gratitude
Today, I am so happy and grateful for...

1 _____   6 _____
2 _____   7 _____
3 _____   8 _____
4 _____   9 _____
5 _____   10 _____

Self-Image
Today, I am...

_____

_____

_____

Inspired Action
Today, I take these actions towards my goals...

1 _____   4 _____
2 _____   5 _____
3 _____   6 _____

Sending Love
Today, I send love to these people in my life...

1 _____
2 _____
3 _____

Powerful Positive Affirmation

I LIKE KNOWING THAT ALL RESULTS
I SEEK ARE EASILY ACHIEVABLE.

Gratitude

Today, I am so happy and grateful for...

1 _____   6 _____

2 _____   7 _____

3 _____   8 _____

4 _____   9 _____

5 _____   10 _____

Self-Image

Today, I am...

_____

_____

_____

Inspired Action

Today, I take these actions towards my goals...

1 _____   4 _____

2 _____   5 _____

3 _____   6 _____

Sending Love

Today, I send love to these people in my life...

1 _____

2 _____

3 _____

Powerful Positive Affirmation

I KNOW IT IS MY DESTINY TO FEEL GOOD.

Gratitude
Today, I am so happy and grateful for...

1 _____   6 _____

2 _____   7 _____

3 _____   8 _____

4 _____   9 _____

5 _____ 10 _____

Self-Image
Today, I am...

_____

_____

_____

Inspired Action
Today, I take these actions towards my goals...

1 _____   4 _____

2 _____   5 _____

3 _____   6 _____

Sending Love
Today, I send love to these people in my life...

1 _____

2 _____

3 _____

Powerful Positive Affirmation

I LOVE KNOWING THAT JOY IS SIMPLY A CHOICE.

Gratitude
Today, I am so happy and grateful for...

1 _____   6 _____
2 _____   7 _____
3 _____   8 _____
4 _____   9 _____
5 _____   10 _____

Self-Image
Today, I am...

_____

_____

_____

Inspired Action
Today, I take these actions towards my goals...

1 _____   4 _____
2 _____   5 _____
3 _____   6 _____

Sending Love
Today, I send love to these people in my life...

1 _____
2 _____
3 _____

Powerful Positive Affirmation

I WAS DESTINED TO A LIFE OF FULFILLMENT AND NEVER-ENDING JOY.

Gratitude

Today, I am so happy and grateful for...

1 _____
2 _____
3 _____
4 _____
5 _____

6 _____
7 _____
8 _____
9 _____
10 _____

Self-Image

Today, I am...

_____

_____

_____

Inspired Action

Today, I take these actions towards my goals...

1 _____
2 _____
3 _____

4 _____
5 _____
6 _____

Sending Love

Today, I send love to these people in my life...

1 _____
2 _____
3 _____

Powerful Positive Affirmation

WHERE I AM IS CONSTANTLY CHANGING TO SOMETHING BETTER.

Gratitude

Today, I am so happy and grateful for...

1 _____   6 _____
2 _____   7 _____
3 _____   8 _____
4 _____   9 _____
5 _____   10 _____

Self-Image

Today, I am...

_____
_____
_____

Inspired Action

Today, I take these actions towards my goals...

1 _____   4 _____
2 _____   5 _____
3 _____   6 _____

Sending Love

Today, I send love to these people in my life...

1 _____
2 _____
3 _____

Powerful Positive Affirmation

IN MY APPRECIATION, I ALLOW MYSELF
TO RECEIVE WONDERFUL THINGS.

Gratitude
Today, I am so happy and grateful for...

1 _____   6 _____

2 _____   7 _____

3 _____   8 _____

4 _____   9 _____

5 _____   10 _____

Self-Image
Today, I am...

_____

_____

_____

Inspired Action
Today, I take these actions towards my goals...

1 _____   4 _____

2 _____   5 _____

3 _____   6 _____

Sending Love
Today, I send love to these people in my life...

1 _____

2 _____

3 _____

Powerful Positive Affirmation

I AM THE CREATOR OF MY MOOD, THEREFORE I AM THE CREATOR OF MY DAY.

Gratitude
Today, I am so happy and grateful for...

1 _____   6 _____
2 _____   7 _____
3 _____   8 _____
4 _____   9 _____
5 _____   10 _____

Self-Image
Today, I am...

_____

_____

_____

Inspired Action
Today, I take these actions towards my goals...

1 _____   4 _____
2 _____   5 _____
3 _____   6 _____

Sending Love
Today, I send love to these people in my life...

1 _____
2 _____
3 _____

Powerful Positive Affirmation

IF I WANT IT, I CAN ATTRACT IT. SIMPLE.

Gratitude
Today, I am so happy and grateful for...

1 _____   6 _____

2 _____   7 _____

3 _____   8 _____

4 _____   9 _____

5 _____   10 _____

Self-Image
Today, I am...

_____

_____

_____

Inspired Action
Today, I take these actions towards my goals...

1 _____   4 _____

2 _____   5 _____

3 _____   6 _____

Sending Love
Today, I send love to these people in my life...

1 _____

2 _____

3 _____

Powerful Positive Affirmation

I LOVE KNOWING THAT IT DOESN'T MATTER WHAT'S GOING ON RIGHT NOW, BECAUSE I CAN KEEP TELLING A NEW STORY.

Gratitude
Today, I am so happy and grateful for...

1 _____   6 _____
2 _____   7 _____
3 _____   8 _____
4 _____   9 _____
5 _____   10 _____

Self-Image
Today, I am...

_____

_____

_____

Inspired Action
Today, I take these actions towards my goals...

1 _____   4 _____
2 _____   5 _____
3 _____   6 _____

Sending Love
Today, I send love to these people in my life...

1 _____
2 _____
3 _____

Powerful Positive Affirmation

I'M ON THE PATH. THE PATH IS UNFOLDING. IT WILL REVEAL ITSELF TO ME IN ITS PERFECT TIMING, AND ALL IS REALLY WELL.

Gratitude
Today, I am so happy and grateful for...

1 _____   6 _____

2 _____   7 _____

3 _____   8 _____

4 _____   9 _____

5 _____   10 _____

Self-Image
Today, I am...

_____

_____

_____

Inspired Action
Today, I take these actions towards my goals...

1 _____   4 _____

2 _____   5 _____

3 _____   6 _____

Sending Love
Today, I send love to these people in my life...

1 _____

2 _____

3 _____

Powerful Positive Affirmation

I AM WHOLE, STRONG, HAPPY AND SURE.

Gratitude
Today, I am so happy and grateful for...

1 _____   6 _____
2 _____   7 _____
3 _____   8 _____
4 _____   9 _____
5 _____   10 _____

Self-Image
Today, I am...

_____

_____

_____

Inspired Action
Today, I take these actions towards my goals...

1 _____   4 _____
2 _____   5 _____
3 _____   6 _____

Sending Love
Today, I send love to these people in my life...

1 _____
2 _____
3 _____

Powerful Positive Affirmation

I HAVE THE ABILITY TO FOCUS.
I HAVE THE ABILITY TO PUT MY
THOUGHTS WHERE THEY FEEL BEST.

Gratitude

Today, I am so happy and grateful for...

1 _____   6 _____

2 _____   7 _____

3 _____   8 _____

4 _____   9 _____

5 _____   10 _____

Self-Image

Today, I am...

_____

_____

_____

Inspired Action

Today, I take these actions towards my goals...

1 _____   4 _____

2 _____   5 _____

3 _____   6 _____

Sending Love

Today, I send love to these people in my life...

1 _____

2 _____

3 _____

Powerful Positive Affirmation

I LOVE ME. I AM LOVABLE. I AM LOVED.

Gratitude

Today, I am so happy and grateful for...

1 _____   6 _____

2 _____   7 _____

3 _____   8 _____

4 _____   9 _____

5 _____   10 _____

Self-Image

Today, I am...

_____

_____

_____

Inspired Action

Today, I take these actions towards my goals...

1 _____   4 _____

2 _____   5 _____

3 _____   6 _____

Sending Love

Today, I send love to these people in my life...

1 _____

2 _____

3 _____

Powerful Positive Affirmation

I CHOOSE TO FEEL GOOD.

Gratitude
Today, I am so happy and grateful for...

1 _____   6 _____
2 _____   7 _____
3 _____   8 _____
4 _____   9 _____
5 _____   10 _____

Self-Image
Today, I am...

_____
_____
_____

Inspired Action
Today, I take these actions towards my goals...

1 _____   4 _____
2 _____   5 _____
3 _____   6 _____

Sending Love
Today, I send love to these people in my life...

1 _____
2 _____
3 _____

Powerful Positive Affirmation

I CREATE MY LIFE ON A QUANTUM LEVEL. THERE ARE ENDLESS OPPORTUNITIES.

Gratitude

Today, I am so happy and grateful for...

1 _____   6 _____

2 _____   7 _____

3 _____   8 _____

4 _____   9 _____

5 _____   10 _____

Self-Image

Today, I am...

_____

_____

_____

Inspired Action

Today, I take these actions towards my goals...

1 _____   4 _____

2 _____   5 _____

3 _____   6 _____

Sending Love

Today, I send love to these people in my life...

1 _____

2 _____

3 _____

Powerful Positive Affirmation

I HAVE A HEALTHY BODY, TRANQUIL MIND
AND A VIBRANT SOUL.

Gratitude

Today, I am so happy and grateful for...

1 _____ 6 _____

2 _____ 7 _____

3 _____ 8 _____

4 _____ 9 _____

5 _____ 10 _____

Self-Image
Today, I am...

_____

_____

_____

Inspired Action
Today, I take these actions towards my goals...

1 _____ 4 _____

2 _____ 5 _____

3 _____ 6 _____

Sending Love
Today, I send love to these people in my life...

1 _____

2 _____

3 _____

Powerful Positive Affirmation

I LOVE THE FACT THAT SO MANY PEOPLE HAVE FAITH IN ME.

Gratitude

Today, I am so happy and grateful for...

1 _____   6 _____
2 _____   7 _____
3 _____   8 _____
4 _____   9 _____
5 _____   10 _____

Self-Image
Today, I am...

_____

_____

_____

Inspired Action
Today, I take these actions towards my goals...

1 _____   4 _____
2 _____   5 _____
3 _____   6 _____

Sending Love
Today, I send love to these people in my life...

1 _____
2 _____
3 _____

Powerful Positive Affirmation

I CREATE HAPPINESS BY APPRECIATING
THE LITTLE THINGS IN LIFE.

Gratitude

Today, I am so happy and grateful for...

1 _____ 6 _____

2 _____ 7 _____

3 _____ 8 _____

4 _____ 9 _____

5 _____ 10 _____

Self-Image

Today, I am...

_____

_____

_____

Inspired Action

Today, I take these actions towards my goals...

1 _____ 4 _____

2 _____ 5 _____

3 _____ 6 _____

Sending Love

Today, I send love to these people in my life...

1 _____

2 _____

3 _____

Powerful Positive Affirmation

I EMBRACE THE RHYTHM OF LIFE
AND LET IT UNFOLD.

Gratitude
Today, I am so happy and grateful for...

1 _____   6 _____
2 _____   7 _____
3 _____   8 _____
4 _____   9 _____
5 _____   10 _____

Self-Image
Today, I am...

_____

_____

_____

Inspired Action
Today, I take these actions towards my goals...

1 _____   4 _____
2 _____   5 _____
3 _____   6 _____

Sending Love
Today, I send love to these people in my life...

1 _____

2 _____

3 _____

Powerful Positive Affirmation

I FOCUS ON ACTION TO CREATE THE LIFE I WANT. THE SMALLEST STEP CAN END YEARS OF STAGNATION.

Gratitude
Today, I am so happy and grateful for...

1 _____   6 _____
2 _____   7 _____
3 _____   8 _____
4 _____   9 _____
5 _____   10 _____

Self-Image
Today, I am...

_____

_____

_____

Inspired Action
Today, I take these actions towards my goals...

1 _____   4 _____
2 _____   5 _____
3 _____   6 _____

Sending Love
Today, I send love to these people in my life...

1 _____
2 _____
3 _____

Powerful Positive Affirmation

I KNOW MY INTUITION WILL ALWAYS TAKE ME IN THE RIGHT DIRECTION.

Gratitude

Today, I am so happy and grateful for...

1 _____   6 _____

2 _____   7 _____

3 _____   8 _____

4 _____   9 _____

5 _____   10 _____

Self-Image

Today, I am...

_____

_____

_____

Inspired Action

Today, I take these actions towards my goals...

1 _____   4 _____

2 _____   5 _____

3 _____   6 _____

Sending Love

Today, I send love to these people in my life...

1 _____

2 _____

3 _____

Powerful Positive Affirmation

I CAN BECOME ANYTHING I PUT MY MIND TO.

Gratitude
Today, I am so happy and grateful for...

1 _____ 6 _____
2 _____ 7 _____
3 _____ 8 _____
4 _____ 9 _____
5 _____ 10 _____

Self-Image
Today, I am...

_____

_____

_____

Inspired Action
Today, I take these actions towards my goals...

1 _____ 4 _____
2 _____ 5 _____
3 _____ 6 _____

Sending Love
Today, I send love to these people in my life...

1 _____
2 _____
3 _____

Powerful Positive Affirmation

I ALWAYS GIVE WHEN I CAN BECAUSE I KNOW IT ALWAYS COMES BACK.

Gratitude

Today, I am so happy and grateful for...

1 _____ 6 _____

2 _____ 7 _____

3 _____ 8 _____

4 _____ 9 _____

5 _____ 10 _____

Self-Image

Today, I am...

_____

_____

_____

Inspired Action

Today, I take these actions towards my goals...

1 _____ 4 _____

2 _____ 5 _____

3 _____ 6 _____

Sending Love

Today, I send love to these people in my life...

1 _____

2 _____

3 _____

Powerful Positive Affirmation

I LOVE THE CREATIVE ENERGY
THAT FLOWS THROUGH ME.

Gratitude
Today, I am so happy and grateful for...

1 _____   6 _____
2 _____   7 _____
3 _____   8 _____
4 _____   9 _____
5 _____   10 _____

Self-Image
Today, I am...

_____
_____
_____

Inspired Action
Today, I take these actions towards my goals...

1 _____   4 _____
2 _____   5 _____
3 _____   6 _____

Sending Love
Today, I send love to these people in my life...

1 _____
2 _____
3 _____

Powerful Positive Affirmation

I LIVE FOR A SPIRITUAL PURPOSE.

Gratitude

Today, I am so happy and grateful for...

1 _____   6 _____
2 _____   7 _____
3 _____   8 _____
4 _____   9 _____
5 _____   10 _____

Self-Image

Today, I am...

_____

_____

_____

Inspired Action

Today, I take these actions towards my goals...

1 _____   4 _____
2 _____   5 _____
3 _____   6 _____

Sending Love

Today, I send love to these people in my life...

1 _____
2 _____
3 _____

Powerful Positive Affirmation

I GIVE MYSELF THE GIFT OF POSITIVITY
BY FOCUSING ON WHAT I WANT.

Gratitude

Today, I am so happy and grateful for...

1 _____   6 _____
2 _____   7 _____
3 _____   8 _____
4 _____   9 _____
5 _____   10 _____

Self-Image

Today, I am...

_____

_____

_____

Inspired Action

Today, I take these actions towards my goals...

1 _____   4 _____
2 _____   5 _____
3 _____   6 _____

Sending Love

Today, I send love to these people in my life...

1 _____

2 _____

3 _____

Powerful Positive Affirmation

I LOVE MYSELF, ALL OF MYSELF.

Gratitude

Today, I am so happy and grateful for...

1 _____   6 _____

2 _____   7 _____

3 _____   8 _____

4 _____   9 _____

5 _____   10 _____

Self-Image

Today, I am...

_____

_____

_____

Inspired Action

Today, I take these actions towards my goals...

1 _____   4 _____

2 _____   5 _____

3 _____   6 _____

Sending Love

Today, I send love to these people in my life...

1 _____

2 _____

3 _____

Powerful Positive Affirmation

I AM MADE OF LOVE.

Gratitude

Today, I am so happy and grateful for...

1 _____   6 _____
2 _____   7 _____
3 _____   8 _____
4 _____   9 _____
5 _____   10 _____

Self-Image
Today, I am...

_____
_____
_____

Inspired Action
Today, I take these actions towards my goals...

1 _____   4 _____
2 _____   5 _____
3 _____   6 _____

Sending Love
Today, I send love to these people in my life...

1 _____
2 _____
3 _____

Powerful Positive Affirmation

I LIVE IN A FRIENDLY UNIVERSE, FULL OF LOVE, JOY, HAPPINESS AND ABUNDANCE.

Gratitude

Today, I am so happy and grateful for...

1 _____   6 _____

2 _____   7 _____

3 _____   8 _____

4 _____   9 _____

5 _____   10 _____

Self-Image

Today, I am...

_____

_____

_____

Inspired Action

Today, I take these actions towards my goals...

1 _____   4 _____

2 _____   5 _____

3 _____   6 _____

Sending Love

Today, I send love to these people in my life...

1 _____

2 _____

3 _____

Powerful Positive Affirmation

EVERYDAY, I AM HEALTHIER, HAPPIER AND MORE VIBRANT.

Gratitude
Today, I am so happy and grateful for...

1 _____   6 _____
2 _____   7 _____
3 _____   8 _____
4 _____   9 _____
5 _____   10 _____

Self-Image
Today, I am...

_____
_____
_____

Inspired Action
Today, I take these actions towards my goals...

1 _____   4 _____
2 _____   5 _____
3 _____   6 _____

Sending Love
Today, I send love to these people in my life...

1 _____
2 _____
3 _____

Powerful Positive Affirmation

I AM BEAUTIFUL ON THE INSIDE AND OUT.

Day   Month   Year

Gratitude
Today, I am so happy and grateful for...

1 _____   6 _____
2 _____   7 _____
3 _____   8 _____
4 _____   9 _____
5 _____   10 _____

Self-Image
Today, I am...

_____
_____
_____

Inspired Action
Today, I take these actions towards my goals...

1 _____   4 _____
2 _____   5 _____
3 _____   6 _____

Sending Love
Today, I send love to these people in my life...

1 _____
2 _____
3 _____

Powerful Positive Affirmation

I AM A MAGNET FOR LOVE, HAPPINESS, JOY, HEALTH, ENERGY AND ABUNDANCE.

CONGRATULATIONS ON COMPLETING YOUR 365-DAY JOURNEY OF

Gratitude, Positivity & Self-Love!

Keep going on this incredible inner journey of loving your self and loving life! Notice and celebrate the transformations you have experienced on this journey.

I invite you to continue this practice forever and to share the this way of being with others so that they can also enjoy the benefits of this transformational practice.

I celebrate you.
I appreciate you.
May you always be happy.

Printed in Great Britain
by Amazon